Becoming the Person I Was Meant to Be: A Memoir of A Patient's Successful Psychoanalysis

Becoming the Person I Was Meant to Be

A Memoir of A Patient's Successful Psychoanalysis

By H. Penny Mishkin

International Psychoanalytic Books (IPBooks)
New York • http://www.IPBooks.net

Published by IPBooks, Queens, NY
Copyright © 2023 H. Penny Miskhin

ISBN 978-1-956864-52-6

In memory of my beloved grandmother "Nana",
my first guardian angel.
And with deep appreciation and affection for
Dr. Norman Straker, my second.

Table of Contents

Preface

Most books about psychotherapy are written from the clinician's perspective. There is very little written directly from the patient's point of view. This book is intended to provide my perspective as a patient in psychodynamic/psychoanalytic therapy and to illustrate how it transformed my life. It is also intended to guide other individuals to determine what might be the best treatment to help them.

This is especially important because psychoanalysis has re-emerged and become more popular. Recently in March 2023, The New York Times published an elucidating article titled *Not Your Daddy's Freud* about the reemergence of psychoanalysis.[1] Not only are there many more applicants to train to become psychoanalysts, there are many more patients choosing it as well. Psychoanalysis not only transformed my life, it gave me a life that is gratifying, satisfying, and full of pride. I would like the reader to have a very good sense of what my experience was like so they can choose what is the right therapy for themselves. I was delighted to learn that psychoanalysis has been rediscovered and of benefit to

---

1 Berstein, Joseph. "Not Your Daddy's Freud." March 23, 2023 https://www.nytimes.com/2023/03/22/style/freud-psychoanalysis.html

more people. I will forever be grateful for Dr. Norman Straker, the excellent therapist with whom I worked.

There are many forms of psychotherapy. Sometimes psycho-pharmacology with follow up visits to check how the medication is working is enough to improve the individual's functioning. There are also several forms of talk therapy. For example, Cognitive Behavioral Therapy is a type of talk therapy that teaches you to see when your thoughts are inaccurate or negative. It focuses on identifying symptoms and finding solutions for them but does not address where the symptoms come from and why they exist. Talk therapy once or twice a week to discuss things that are of concern to the patient such as coping with a crisis, the loss of a loved one, or even just the anxiety that something like the pandemic produced is enough. I consider psychodynamic/psychoanalytic treatment to go deeper into the personality and character of the individual to determine what is in their way that caused them to seek treatment. I liken it to the gut renovation of an apartment that involves moving walls, restructuring, and transforming the space as opposed to the cosmetics of painting and refinishing floors.

The first time I considered starting therapy was in my freshman year of college when I became very depressed and even for a short time suicidal. I didn't pursue therapy because I did not want to admit to my parents that I wanted help, because I thought they would see me as damaged and defective as I had viewed myself since early childhood. A year later I became anorexic although that is not why I sought therapy. Additionally, I thought that asking for help was a sign of weakness; going for psychiatric help was even more of an admission of weakness. I did not know anyone in therapy and felt that there must be something very wrong with you if you went, which was a common attitude to have in 1967. By my senior year in college, several of my friends were going to therapy at the university's health center. I didn't think there was anything wrong with them, they just wanted some additional help with specific problems in their lives. Consequently, my attitude changed and I gave myself permission to seek help. One of the first things I did the following year when I went to graduate school to earn a PhD in philosophy was to get a referral for psychotherapy from the university's health center. At this point I had received an inheritance from my beloved grandmother that allowed me to pay for therapy myself so I would not have to involve my parents. (I did eventually tell them within a year.)

In the fall of 1971, I started therapy twice a week. I went for eight months until I moved back to my hometown of New York City. I moved back for two reasons: I did not like my graduate school program and I was raped in the spring semester. Before moving, my therapist told me I didn't need to seek therapy once I returned home. (Boy did I have him fooled!) He advised me to call him if I wanted to resume therapy so he could provide a referral.

I spent that summer from mid-May to mid-September 1972 at my parent's home in Greenwich, Connecticut. In June of that summer, I testified in the trial of the men who raped me. They were convicted and sent to prison for 4-7 years, which was considered a long sentence in 1972. This was part of my healing process. The jury's verdict validated my perceptions and despite the defense attorney's attempt to make me out to be a prostitute and liar, the jury believed me and convicted the men of rape and kidnapping. My testimony ensured that they were punished and locked away. This made me feel stronger and less of a victim. It was healing to be believed and justice was served. Once I returned home, I did not discuss the rape with friends or family. Instead, I wanted to feel safe and get on with my life. I volunteered in the art department at a residential school for emotionally disturbed children. In retrospect it was fitting that I was drawn to working with other wounded individuals. The woman who ran the department was very kind and sensitive and I think she saw how fragile I was. As an aside, I'm sure this experience helped pave the way to my becoming an occupational therapist six years later. At the end of the summer, I got my own apartment in Manhattan near where I grew up. I also found a position as a publicity assistant at the publishing company Grosset and Dunlap, the publishers of the *Nancy Drew* and *Hardy Boys* series. Many of the friends I grew up with were still in New York and we spent many evenings together. I went to parties, met new people, and felt I was back on track. To a great extent, though I didn't realize it, I was just going through the motions. I was doing what was expected of me as I had always done. I was traumatized by the rape, however I still had my defenses of dissociation and numbness, which served me well for a while. Two years later I was able to attain a competitively desirable position as an editorial assistant in trade publishing at Random House. Although I loved my job, I found myself severely depressed at times.

That summer when I spent weekends at my parent's home in Greenwich, my mother noticed a change in my mood. She suggested that I go back into therapy, which was an unusual, yet thoughtful and loving comment from her. I agreed with her and contacted my former therapist in Boston who gave me three referrals. He suggested the William Allanson White Institute, Karen Horney Clinic, and the head of the department of psychiatry at Mount Sinai Hospital. I contacted all three but instinctively knew the first two options were not for me. I clearly remember going into an empty office at Random House during my lunch time and contacting the department head at Mount Sinai. He was not taking on new patients but asked me several questions so he could refer me to another psychiatrist. I remember how uncomfortable it was answering questions about why I was seeking therapy. It was excruciating to tell a stranger things I was ashamed of. I told him I had been brutally raped two years earlier, I was depressed, and that I was afraid of sexual intimacy. He was very kind and helpful and spent enough time with me to make a thoughtful referral. He gave me the name of a psychiatrist in private practice, Dr. Norman Straker, and I arranged for a consultation.

CHAPTER 1

———

Beginning

In 1974 it was common practice for a psychiatrist to arrange with a potential new patient for three consultation sessions not only to assess the patient but also to determine whether they would be able to help them. In the first consultation, I was asked what brought me to therapy and what issues I wanted to resolve. I told my analyst that I came from a perfect family and the only thing wrong with it was me. (My family included my parents and my three siblings.) He asked me to elaborate so he could understand why I would make such an unusual statement. In the second consultation, he continued to take a thorough developmental history. Although I did not realize how significant it was at the time, I told him that I had a severe visual impairment in childhood but that when I got contact lenses at age twelve it no longer had an impact. I am so glad he did not accept this at face value. The third of my consultations was on October 12, 1974: Columbus Day three weeks before my 25th birthday. The reason I'm certain of this date is because I remember almost being late to the appointment due to the terrible traffic the parade had created. I recall that session began with my analyst telling me he felt he could help me and imparting his recommendations as well as the ground rules. He recommended that I see him three times a week which took me by surprise. I asked him, "Why three?" believing he must think I was really damaged. He patiently explained that the frequency of sessions was not related to the degree of pathology. Instead, the frequency of visits was related to what would work best for the individual and not the severity of the patient's issues. I accepted this explanation and over the course of my analysis the frequency of sessions varied according to my needs. I also asked him how long the therapy would take. He replied, "It will take as long as it takes." I remember thinking this was an evasive answer but did not challenge it. How I viewed it, we would be done when I was perfect since perfection was my goal. (Within a year I learned how naive that was. I believe I owe much of my perfectionism to my parents. They were very critical and judgemental. For example, one day when I was a teenager my mother said to me unprompted, "Penny, the problem with you is you have no self confidence." I thought to myself *No wonder I have no self confidence, you criticize me all the time!*) I eventually realized that he had not given me an evasive answer and that it is very difficult to predict how long an analysis would last, partly because one's goals may change as the treatment progresses. He asked me, "What's the hurry?" I told him that I wanted to feel better as soon as possible. Quite honestly if he had told me it would take 40 years, I would've run out of his office as fast as I could! He then told me that I would have to pay for sessions whether I attended them or not. I didn't question this policy at the time because I had always been a rule follower and didn't expect to miss any sessions. We also discussed the role of free association and dreams.

I accepted his recommendations and with that acceptance my therapy with Dr. Norman Straker had begun. I cannot imagine a better metaphor for this beginning than the fact that it took place on Columbus Day. Although I didn't realize it at the time, *I had set sail on a journey to discover a new world for myself. I did not realize where I was going, what I would discover, what a difficult journey it would be at times, or where I would finally arrive.*

CHAPTER 2

The First Year

Within the first month of therapy I made enormous progress in the area of sexual intimacy, which also alleviated much of my depression. I was very fortunate to meet a wonderful young man, four years my senior who was very kind and compassionate. In those days when you were dating someone there was a mutual expectation that you would be physically intimate by the third date. Despite being well aware of this, I was reluctant because I was so inexperienced and afraid. Although it was very difficult, I confided in him that I had been raped two years earlier. I explained that this amplified my fears about having a new sexual partner. He was so kind and made me feel so understood that it intensified my affection for him (this was the first man I had ever revealed the rape to). I think my experience with a kind and compassionate analyst, to whom I was revealing very private information, made it possible to recognize that I could do the same with a kind and compassionate boyfriend. Shortly after I confided in him, he arranged for us to go to a lovely inn for the weekend in Connecticut. He had even been thoughtful enough to bring a nice bottle of Cabernet as well as the best eclairs you could find in New York City to make the evening more special. His thoughtfulness and consideration allowed me to overcome my fear and I was able to enjoy sexual intimacy with him. This was a lovely way to lose my virginity. I was a virgin when I was raped but I never considered that the loss of my virginity as I considered it only an act of violence.

Finally overcoming my fear of sexual intimacy helped me realize that it was just the tip of the iceberg. When telling my analyst about the lovely weekend I had had, the discussions and explorations that followed helped me understand that my intimacy issues extended well beyond sex. We discussed the contribution my limited parenting had and how it set me up for remoteness and detachment. We explored how much this stemmed from the fact that appearances were more important to my parents than feelings. I learned from an early age how to present myself and appear better put together than I actually was. I hid my insecurities behind a wall of disconnection and remoteness. As a young child I was well behaved, polite, friendly and well liked by my peers, their parents, and my teachers. As an adult I made a very good impression being attractive, well dressed, and a good conversationalist. For example, I interviewed for jobs very well which is illustrated by my attaining the position of editorial assistant at Random House with one of their best editors. I was able to maintain this appearance in my job because I was skilled at interacting with renowned authors and celebrities both on the phone and in person. My ability to remain distant was an asset in this situation as this job didn't require any intimacy or real expression of emotion. It came naturally to maintain professionalism.

I was inhibited and guarded however, I also maintained my pretenses and charades. Although I was able to fool my first therapist, thank goodness I was not able to fool my analyst. He saw right through me. Free associating and revealing private information was very difficult for me. I was so used to hiding my true feelings from a very early age, that this made it very challenging to free associate, reveal my feelings and almost anything private. For example, I would come at the beginning of the week wanting to reveal something that I was ashamed of but I simply could not do it. I would sputter to my analyst that there was something I wanted to tell him but I was too embarrassed to reveal it. His response was largely silence, the most therapeutic response. The silence was therapeutic because it demonstrated that I was responsible for expressing my feelings and it was not his job to pull it from me. I tried to spit it out but just could not. Most of the session was complete silence. This was excruciating and was repeated at my second session of the week. By the third session, I was so frustrated by the previous ones that I blurted my secret out. I was so ashamed that my secret indicated I was abnormal. Once I did reveal it, my analyst assured me that the "revelation" was not abnormal or particularly unusual. What was unusual was the amount of shame

I felt about it. This was reassuring and provided relief and made it a little easier to open up. This was typical of how my first year in analysis went. Not everything was this difficult to disclose. It was easy to finally discuss the unusual parenting I received and experienced. What an important catharsis this was! We also more easily discussed issues about friends, siblings, and work.

At this point I think it's important to explain the reason I was so ashamed of my thoughts and feelings. I learned this was mainly due to how I was raised and the impact of my severe visual impairment. My parents never discussed their feelings and made it evident they were not interested in mine. I was expected to be happy all the time. Crying or asking for help was taboo. It was quite clear from a very early age that I would not receive comfort. My need for comfort was amplified because of my severe visual impairment. I was bullied and my behavior was often misunderstood and misinterpreted. I kept these experiences to myself because I thought I deserved it, though I didn't know why. Consequently, I never received comfort or understanding that this was not my fault. In turn, my defense mechanism was not to feel my emotions and to hide the visual impairment itself. My parents needed me to be "perfect" and I adopted their point of view, hiding my disability and its consequences as well as I could. This worked well enough until my teen years when I first became depressed.

An excellent example of how disconnected from my feelings I was and how this impacted my relationship with my analyst is my reaction to his vacationing for the entire month of August. In July of that first year, with his August vacation approaching, my analyst asked me what my feelings were about his being away. I said I had none because this was not a big deal and wondered to myself "Why are you asking such a stupid question?" When I told him I had no feelings about this, he probed. Yet I really believed it was of no consequence. As it turned out, I later realized I had a lot of feelings about this. However, I did not come to this realization until he had been gone for about two weeks. I missed him terribly and was very depressed that he was absent. When we resumed therapy in September I had no reluctance in revealing how difficult the month of August had been for me. We had finally begun to penetrate the numbness and disconnection that had been my modus operandi until then.

CHAPTER 3

Second Year

I eagerly anticipated our reunion after labor day. Although I was still guarded, it was easier for me to express my feelings and reveal how distressing his absence had been. We began to explore why I expected his absence to be of no consequence. We discussed the impact of my parent's remoteness. At times their remoteness was expressed by how frequently they traveled. For example, when I was three years old they were on vacation for a six week European cruise. My siblings and I, who were nine, seven, three (that's me), and two years old, were left in the capable but unaffectionate hands of our nanny. I came down with pneumonia while they were away and my nanny contacted them to let them know how sick I was. At home there was so much anxiety about my illness that it impacted my siblings, especially my older brother. He told me it was very scary for him because my fever had reached over 105 degrees. My parents did not disrupt their vacation and did not return home to take care of me, provide comfort, or alleviate my siblings' anxiety. (Their indifference foreshadowed how they responded after I was raped.)

I don't recall ever missing my parents. For example, I never experienced homesickness when I went to sleep away camp even when I was as young as six years old. I recall witnessing the homesickness of my peers. Although I noticed it, I did not comprehend it. This continued for the following nine years that I attended my eight week sleep away camp in the summers. By the time I was thirteen, I even told my parents that it was unnecessary for them to come to visiting day as their presence or absence was of no consequence. (I knew if they didn't come to visit me they wouldn't visit my brother's camp which was fifteen minutes away. I asked my younger brother how he felt about this and he didn't care whether they visited either.)

If I never missed my parents, why would I think I would miss my analyst?

My siblings were treated exactly as I was. When I was the third to go away to camp at age six, my younger brother Ricky experienced what it was like to be an "only child" for the first time. One would think despite missing his siblings, he would've enjoyed the extra attention he got as the "only child." That was not the case. Instead, he was very "homesick" for his siblings because he did not receive any extra attention from our parents. He begged to be sent to sleep away camp for the following summer because he had been so lonely. When Ricky attended camp the following year, my older brother Joe said that it was his worst summer at camp because he felt the need to look after his younger brother. Ricky had only completed kindergarten and was not even able to write letters home or read any letters sent to him. When I asked my brother Joe if he had ever been homesick, he told me he'd never experienced missing them. When I asked my sister, she told me it was the other way around and that she would cry when it was time to leave camp and go home.

A further illustration of their unusual parenting style is that once we had returned from camp there were still two weeks before we resumed school. For the first week, they spent their time at our country club, which had the equivalent of hotel rooms, while the four of us stayed at a nearby motel with our nanny. We spent at least one week at the motel until we needed to return to the city to prepare for the new school year. (Our country club allowed children, provided there was parental supervision. This did not interest my parents.) Nevertheless, the four of us really enjoyed staying at the motel because it had a swimming pool and we ate breakfast and lunch out at a restaurant each day. My parents thought putting us at the motel was a treat for us all. They were using a special place as a substitute for their presence. In other words, what mattered more was *what* we were doing rather than *who* we were doing it with. For the first several years of my analysis I often emphasized the place or activity rather than the importance of who I was with. It became an important theme in my analysis that I focused more on what I did rather than who I did it with. This is an example of what analysis is like. The analyst listens very intently to what you are saying; it's a special kind of listening that requires expertise. As a result of my analysts' careful listening, he would discern the underlying issue that was at play. We went over all of this in such detail so I wouldn't continue repeating the patterns of my past.

My parents' absence didn't have a conscious impact on me because I really enjoyed staying at the motel, eating out, and the company of my brothers and sister. They did however take us to dinner several nights a week, which we all really enjoyed as dinner was one of our favorite times as a family. My siblings and I were accustomed to this kind of remoteness and lack of involvement from our parents so we didn't think there was anything unusual about this entire experience. No wonder I did not expect to miss my analyst when he was away for a month. When I casually mentioned the motel stay to my analyst, he was shocked for two reasons. First that my parents would do this and second that I thought there was nothing remarkable about it. He was stunned by the whole situation. It took a while for me to understand how remote and detached my parents were and how that pervaded my childhood. No wonder it took so long for him to convince me that this was very unusual parental behavior. He would tell me that he'd never heard of such a thing and I would reply "But it was so much fun!" We spent many sessions on this because I was so accustomed to the way my parents treated us and couldn't see how it represented their detachment. It took a lot of work for me to eventually understand what unusual parenting this was. However, the silver lining was that it created very strong bonds between my siblings and me. This filled the gap that my parents created.

When my niece was 15 she said the following: "You all say that you were very close growing up. On the other hand, you've also all told me that you never discussed your feelings with each other. How could you be close if you never discussed your feelings?" I told her that was a very interesting question. (Today she is a very successful clinical psychologist.) I thought about it and told her that most of the time I could just sense when one of my siblings was sad or upset. Since feelings were not discussed in my family, instead of asking them to talk about it I just was kinder to them. For example, if I sensed something was wrong I might let my sister choose the television program or go into the kitchen and bring her a treat. My brother might tell me jokes or ask to play a game to cheer me up. This is how we showed our love and care for each other.

Many years later when I reconnected with an old friend, we were comparing childhood memories. I asked what she and her mother remembered about my family since our families lived in the same building. She told me her mother still remembered an evening playing Canasta with my mother at her home. My nanny called to tell my mother that one of her children was sick. My mother said with annoyance, "Why are you calling me? You should call the doctor." and continued her card game despite the fact that her children were only a short elevator ride away. My mother's friend remembered this because she was astonished at how unresponsive my mother had been. When I learned this story, I found it incomprehensible as well as heartless on my mother's part. When I related this vignette to my analyst, he had insight into my mother's behavior based on what he had learned about her from me. (My analyst understood my mother better than anyone I knew.) He explained that my mother likely felt insecure and helpless in taking care of or providing comfort to a sick child. He made the following analogy: *had your nanny called your mother to tell her that the sink was leaking, she would've responded "Why are you calling me? Call the plumber."* Which would have made sense.

Hopefully these examples explain why I grew up feeling neither of my parents loved me and why I used the defense mechanism of disconnection and numbness to mitigate it. This is consistent with my response to my analyst: "Who, me? Miss *you?*" Although I have no doubt other issues came up in that second year, it was dominated by exploring the unusual and at times incomprehensible parenting I experienced. Although my analyst did not take an August vacation as a therapeutic technique, it proved to be very therapeutic and put me in touch with how detached I was from my feelings, my parents, and him.

CHAPTER 4

The Impact of My Severe Visual Impairment

My limited parenting was not the only trauma that contributed to my being shy, inhibited, and numb. Equally important was that I was born with a visual impairment: a severe case of a condition called pathological myopia, which today is also referred to as degenerative myopia. Pathological myopia is not at all like regular myopia. It is a degenerative disease of the eye that is caused by having very elongated eyeballs as opposed to round ones. I was diagnosed with this condition when I was 2 years old. Because the eyeballs are so elongated it damages the retina and causes the loss of retinal cells, and in my case it was so severe that I'd never had normal retinas. I wore coke bottle thick glasses from the age of two to the age of 12 when I got contact lenses. Most people, including myself, assume that if you're wearing glasses you are fully corrected. After all, that's what glasses are for. However, that is not always the case. I was only able to be corrected to 20/100 vision because of the damage to my retinas, which is the equivalent to being able to read only the second line of the eye chart. Without my glasses I wouldn't even know the chart was there. Because people assumed I was fully corrected, my low vision disability was invisible. My behavior was often misunderstood because no one knew how poorly I saw. In addition, I knew I was different but I did not want anyone else to know I was different. Consequently, I worked very hard to seem like everyone else and to keep my impairment a secret. This was exhausting so there were times I melted down at home because I simply could not maintain this fiction. Today I would have had a formal diagnosis of being a low vision child, which would have informed my teachers and family that I had a disability and provided me with accommodations. This might have prevented my feeling of having to hide my disability and feeling ashamed of myself. For example, my siblings were completely unaware that I had a disability. They knew I had poor eyesight but they felt that when I was wearing my glasses I saw the way they did, which was not true. Dr. Richard Hertel writes poignantly about the trauma of a severe visual impairment in childhood, "Children with visual problems cannot see the ego trauma caused by looking through their damaged eyes. Significant others usually do not see the children's trauma either. Thus, a silent, insidious undermining of the self-ensues." [2] This certainly was the case for me; although I was completely unaware of it

---

2 Hertel, Richard. "Analyzing the Traumatic Impact of Childhood Visual Impairment."- *Journal of the American Psychoanalytic Association,* U.S. National Library of Medicine, pubmed.ncbi.nlm.nih.gov/14596566

until my analysis. One way this was manifested was that my eyes constantly played tricks on me and I was often mistaken about what I was seeing. This undermined my confidence in my ability to perceive things correctly, both visually and emotionally. This was so embedded in my psyche as shown when I visited my elderly mother in the hospital after her hip replacement surgery, she was still hallucinating from the medication. My sister and I knew she was hallucinating because she told us to make an appointment for her with the hairdresser. My sister, not wanting to upset her, went along with this and said "Mom, I'll make the appointment but why do you need to have your hair done?" My mother replied, "I must have it done because I was invited to Queen Elizabeth's birthday party." She then turns to me and asks me why my hair was orange. I turned to my sister and said, "Phyl, is my hair really orange?" My sister said "No!" We both laughed and I quickly realized that even when something was as outrageous as that, my instinct was to automatically accept my mother's and others' perception over mine. Clearly this was a holdover from my childhood. I'm laughing even as I write this now.

This is also reflected in the comment I made to my analyst during the consultation sessions that my poor eyesight had no further impact once I got hard contact lenses at age 12. The reality was that my low vision continued to have an impact throughout my life. I was living in two worlds because I could not wear my contact lenses 24 hours a day. When I took them out I was in a blind world, which posed its challenges especially when I was in an unfamiliar environment and needed to get to a bathroom to reinsert them. When I removed my lenses and was functionally blind, it was very important to me to hide this. I did not want anyone to know how impaired I was because I was ashamed of it. For example, when I was 25 and traveling with my boyfriend that summer in Europe, at times we stayed in hotels where there was a communal bathroom but not one in our room. I had to remove my contact lenses at night but to reinsert them I needed a bathroom. One option was to ask my boyfriend to take me to the bathroom, however I did not want him to know how limited I was. As far back as I can remember, I consciously was aware that I never wanted anyone to pity me or feel sorry for me. Although it wasn't easy I was so determined to keep the extent of my visual impairment a secret that I bravely managed to find the bathroom by myself despite the risks. It saddens me now to recognize that I didn't give myself credit for how well I functioned with such a severe impairment. It was only through my analysis that I learned to be proud of such accomplishments rather than being ashamed of being imperfect.

When I told my analyst how ashamed I was of my impairment and how well I compensated to keep it hidden, he questioned why I was so humiliated rather than acknowledging how well I functioned. He also wondered why I didn't ask for more help. I told him I was taught not to ask for help as it was considered a sign of weakness. This was something we came back to frequently over the years and I came to understand it was ingrained in me that asking for help was a sign of weakness. If I asked for help I would feel humiliated. We also discussed how differently disability was viewed when I was growing up. My disability was truly invisible, not only because society didn't recognize it but because I went so out of my way to align myself with the cultural point of view. When I was growing up, it was not unusual to feel ashamed of having a disability. Individuals with disabilities were stigmatized and often considered second class citizens. There was no legislation as there is now with the Americans With Disabilities Act to protect us. Individuals with disabilities, especially children, were usually hidden. For example, children with physical disabilities such as cerebral palsy, spina bifida, down syndrome, and blindness were usually institutionalized and hidden away. My vision continually deteriorated as I aged and my ophthalmologist thought I was going blind. My parents and I were not told this explicitly, but I think we all feared this because every time I saw the eye doctor my vision had declined. It was natural for us to think I could be going blind. It was very important for me to hide my disability so I would not be sent away to an institution.

My parents and I never discussed this (denial by us all) until I was 42 years old and my father was terminally ill. I'm not sure why I brought it up, however I clearly remember being in the family room where my father was lying on his favorite couch with my mother sitting beside him. I don't know what prompted me to ask them both if they had thought I was going blind when I was growing up. I told them that when I visited Dr. Bloomenthal when I was 27 to review my records (my analysis made me curious about the nature of my impairment as a child) I asked him if he had feared that I was going blind when I was younger. He very honestly told me he had because of how rapidly my eyes were deteriorating between the ages of 2 and 12. I also asked if he had ever told my parents this. He had not. When I related this to my parents, the expressions on their faces told me how relieved they were and it was palpable. I didn't ask them why they were so relieved because I inferred that their fears of my going blind were validated, yet they were relieved they never came true. Although these fears were unspoken, they were worried about me when I was growing up. Throughout the rest of their lives, my eyes had stopped deteriorating and they no longer had to fear I would go blind. I told them I knew they had done everything possible to give me the best vision I could have. In my analysis, I also came to understand how frequently my mother worried about my vision although she almost never expressed it in words. For example, she was very concerned about whether I had adequate vision to drive. Her fear was justified as I did get into a minor accident when I was 18. Though I met the vision standards to get a driver's license, she called my eye doctor to get his opinion. He told her to let me drive, however not with the radio on to avoid distraction. Another example that was a frequent occurrence was when I would hold a menu or book close to my eyes to read it, she would frown at me with a look of what I *thought* was disgust. I didn't know what I did to elicit this but I came to realize in analysis that she wasn't disgusted with me but was upset at the need for me to hold the book so close which reminded her of how impaired I was. She wanted to believe that my eyes were fine and any reminders of my impairment filled her with fear. What I didn't realize at the time was that this was an expression of love. It was such a relief for me to recognize that she wasn't disapproving of me, she was upset and disapproving of any diminished vision I still had. Another memory that comes to mind was when I was 22. I was in my bedroom reading when I thought I saw an ant crawling across the pages. I kept hitting the book to kill the ant without any success. Finally it occurred to me that it might not be an ant that I was seeing. I closed my right eye, and with only my left eye there was no ant on the page. When I closed my left eye and looked with my right, the ant was there. I repeated this to become certain that there was no ant and it must have something to do with my eyes. I went into my parent's bedroom to tell my mother about this new phenomenon and she reasonably panicked. Coincidentally, two of her friend's daughters had recently had retinal detachments and she was concerned the same was happening to me. The next morning she called both of her friends to get the name of the best eye doctor for this condition in New York City. I immediately got an appointment and was examined by a renowned ophthalmologist who was head of the department at Mount Sinai hospital. As upset as she had been, she did not accompany me to the appointment. (I've worked with parents like my mother who felt that once they had brought their child to me, they thought I would "fix" them and there was nothing more for them to do. They felt their role was to find the best physician or therapist and then their job was done.) I was thoroughly examined and he determined that all I had was a floater, which is a very common experience not only for people with poor vision but for everyone. What was unusual was that I had not developed floaters sooner. When I was a little girl, at every visit my ophthalmologist asked me if I saw spots before my eyes. I found this to be a very strange question and wondered whether he thought I was crazy. (When he asked me this, I had envisioned spots that resembled polka dots.) Once I had the floater diagnosed, I suddenly realized that is what he had been referring to.

These memories indicate how abnormal my vision was and the accompanying fears. However, I did not know what "normal" vision was. I remember telling my analyst that when I played tennis I could not tell whether my ball was in or out when it was close to the line on the other side of the court. He said, "Penny, no one can tell. That's why there are linesmen in tennis tournaments." I had never considered this and his comment was a relief that made me feel less impaired. Because I had never seen 20/20,

I thought 20/20 vision meant superhuman vision because relative to the way I saw, it was.

Part of what occurred in my analysis was his correcting the misunderstandings I had because of my poor vision. This not only occurred with my eyesight, it also occurred in my relationships with friends, family, and him. There were times when I had a disagreement with a friend or family member and I would dig my heels in that I was right and they were wrong. At times like this I wish I'd had a linesman. My analyst couldn't be absolutely sure what happened with my friend or family member, however he would know what happened in his office between the two of us. He would provide his point of view, which I often felt was critical and I disagreed. I would insist that my perspective on the issue was correct and he would explain my faulty reasoning. Our conversation would go something like this: he would insist on my faulty reasoning and I'd say *no you're wrong*. He would then try to make his point in a different way so I would understand it and I would again say *NO! You're wrong*. It was the equivalent of him saying the ball was in and my insisting the ball was out. This made me angry and it would've been helpful to have a referee! I so hated being wrong or misinterpreting things. I felt criticized and would become angry. Although he wasn't 100% correct all the time, he was *usually* correct. I did not want to admit that because I did not want to admit I was wrong. To me, being wrong was like being blind.

This is an excellent example of what analysis is like. The immediacy of the relationship was relied on to help me understand my misconceptions. These kinds of instances happen frequently in an analysis and one experience builds on the other to allow for growth, self understanding, and ultimately transformation. Eventually I understood that it was so painful to feel that my perception of what was taking place was wrong, which resonated with feeling blind, that I was not open to a fuller understanding of what was actually taking place between the two of us. This process was an essential aspect of my analysis.

CHAPTER 5

From the Chair to the Couch and Back

One day at lunch with my mother she commented on what an easy baby her latest grandchild was. I asked her what I was like as a baby. She replied, "You were an easy baby until you were about one when you became fussy and difficult" which was how she and my family viewed me from then on. She attributed this to my having a boil lanced on my nose. When I mentioned her comment in my next therapy session, he asked me what I thought about this. *What, Why, When,* and *Where* questions helped us probe how memories could help me understand my past. I free associated and realized that around the time she found me fussy and difficult was when I would've started to walk. As a baby I would've been held close enough in someone's arms that I could see the face of who was holding me. Then when I was crawling I would've been on the floor with objects much closer to me so I could see them. Once I started walking, people and objects were at a further distance and I would not have seen obstacles in my way. What made the most sense to me was that I became fussy and difficult because of the visual impairment that was not yet diagnosed. I think that these new challenges naturally created anxiety and fear which were understood as fussiness and being difficult. When I was two, my nanny noticed I practically pressed my nose to the television screen to see it. Consequently, she suggested to my mother that I see an ophthalmologist and the diagnosis was made. For the next three years I saw my doctor every three months and at most visits my eyes would be dilated so he could view my retinas. I hated the insertion of the eye drops that dilated my eyes and remember that I had to be pinned down and restrained for them to do this. As I mentioned before, when I was in analysis I became curious about the history of my impairment as we discussed the impact of my poor vision. I reviewed my records with my ophthalmologist. He told me I saw him so frequently because my eyes were deteriorating so rapidly that he was afraid I was going blind. I also asked him why my eyes were patched alternately for two to three years. His answer was that there was no treatment for my condition and he took a shot in the dark hoping that it might help. When I mentioned this in my next session, my analyst asked me what I thought about this. Once again, free association was very helpful. What I realized was it wasn't just the application of the patch that I hated. It was also the fact that they were subjecting the patches on a little girl with very poor vision and making it even worse. No wonder I hated the patch and fought against it. As it turned out, there was no medical evidence to suggest that the patches would work. Wearing them was harmful to my visual and emotional development. It intensified my shyness and probably contributed to my distrust of adults and doctors.

As I mentioned before, despite wearing coke bottle thick glasses my vision was only partially corrected. This too contributed to how I viewed myself and others because my behavior was so often misinterpreted. For example, I might bump into another person and they would get angry at me rather than recognize I just hadn't seen them. When I was about eight years old I was on a school bus and a younger child seated on the other side of the bus and two rows behind started to cry. I was told by other girls that this was my fault and I simply could not understand why I was being blamed. I knew I hadn't said anything to the child. It's possible that my very thick glasses upset her or that I looked at her differently than she was accustomed to because of my severe visual impairment. It's also possible that this was a group of mean girls ganging up on me to make me cry as well, which I did. I was so confused and humiliated because the last thing I would ever have wanted to do was to make another little girl cry.

My siblings misunderstood me because they too thought that my vision was fully corrected. (Originally, I wrote this sentence as "I was fully corrected" and then recognized it was my vision that I was writing about. This further revealed to me how much I associated myself and my eyes as one and the same.) My siblings did not know how much I was compensating for my low vision and therefore did not understand why at times

I was difficult at home. They just thought I had a very moody and difficult personality. Whenever I came back from the eye doctor I was always in a bad mood for several reasons. First, I had gotten news that my eyes had deteriorated and I feared I was one step closer to becoming blind and being institutionalized. This would be an unsettling proposition for anyone. Another reason I was "moody"was that at almost every visit my eyes were dilated and very bright lights were shown into my eyes, which was very painful. To this day I still find it very painful and difficult to cooperate even when I'm making every effort to do so. I imagine that throughout my childhood it would've been even more difficult to cooperate. My mother didn't understand how difficult this was and blamed me for being uncooperative when I really just was unable to cooperate. Incidents like this undermined my sense of self and intensified my feelings of being defective. Although my mother may have been disappointed that I wasn't being cooperative, she wanted me to get the best eye examination as possible to provide me with the best vision that was possible. When I discussed it in my analysis, I came to understand that what felt like cruelty was the best way they knew how to help my vision at the time. Kindness and comfort would've made such a difference in how I understood this experience. Because of our greater understanding of disabilities today, I am confident that my mother would have praised me for how well I endured these difficult examinations in contrast to how I felt I wasn't being good enough. This is at least one of the reasons why I told my analyst that I came from a perfect family except for me.

When I first began analysis I did not lie on the couch. I sat on a chair facing my analyst. Indeed, I didn't even notice the couch was there. When I was volunteering at a psychiatric day treatment center to learn more about Occupational Therapy, I remember hearing from some of my coworkers that they would lay on the couch when they were in therapy. To me this meant they were more advanced as a patient and I wanted to be more like everyone else as I had throughout my life. I brought this up in my next session, and as typically would happen in my analysis, we discussed the reasons why I wanted to move to the couch. When you lie on the couch the analyst is sitting behind you and you are unable to see them. This made me feel very vulnerable. This was almost intolerable for me, though I was determined to stick it out. When he asked me what thoughts came to mind about my discomfort, all my associations were about how uncomfortable I was, partly because I couldn't see him and partly because I felt like I was being examined. He asked me to elaborate. What came to mind was my eye examinations when I was a child. He encouraged me to be more specific. My associations were to the bright lights that were shown in my eyes and it was like reliving that painful period in my life. For at least a month on the couch all my thoughts and associations were about how uncomfortable I was. Ultimately my analyst felt the couch was not advancing my therapy, it was actually interfering with it. He recommended I move back to the chair and once again we discussed the move. I felt moving back to the chair was a demotion but I accepted this because I had come to trust him.

A turning point in my therapy was when he insisted our session was over 15 minutes early. I corrected him and told him we still had 15 minutes left of the session. He was so certain that he was right and I was wrong that I left the session. I was very gullible (just like I had been when my mother hallucinated that my hair was orange) and could easily be convinced to relinquish my point of view. So I left. When I got home there was an apology from him on my answering machine telling me it was his mistake about the time and that I was correct. Having grown up with parents who were "always right", this was breathtaking. I realized he would admit when he made a mistake so I could trust him and know that his recommendations were always what he thought was in my best interest. These first few years I was becoming very attached to him and learned to trust him. In subsequent sessions and periodically throughout my analysis, we explored why I allowed myself to be convinced I was wrong when I knew I wasn't. As a result of these discussions I sometimes went to the other extreme and insisted my point of view was correct and would not consider another.

Lying on the couch made me feel more vulnerable and elicited submissive and powerless feelings that resonated with being raped. It was very helpful and important that we discussed the feelings that lying on the couch elicited. Within a year we had investigated this sufficiently, so I was comfortable to resume lying on the couch and did so thereafter. I recognized the difference between being in the chair and lying on the couch. In the chair, I could see his facial expressions and I'm sure he made attempts to hide them. On the couch, because there is no visual feedback you are in a very different space. The ordinary parts of discourse, such as reading facial expressions, body language, and making eye contact no longer exist. It facilitates free association and expression of your feelings.

CHAPTER 6

Becoming The Therapist I Was Meant Be

Although I loved working at Random House, I realized I wasn't cut out for being an editor and didn't want to work as an editorial assistant all my life. It was a glorified secretarial position with some wonderful perks. For example, going to book parties, movie screenings, meeting Paul McCartney and other celebrities. I discussed this in therapy of course, because I knew I wanted to change my career but didn't know what I wanted to change it to. As a result of this discussion, I recognized that I should go for career counseling which proved to be very helpful. I remember taking various tests that would elucidate my interests and what careers I could apply them to. What became evident was that I wanted to work in a "helping" profession. There were many options. I wanted a career that had its own professional identity, including its own professional journal and organization. Three professions were suggested to me: social work, physical therapy, and occupational therapy. After I left Random House, I spent the following year volunteering at various hospitals to learn more about each of these professions. Although I did not know what occupational therapy was at the time, once I learned about it I chose it because it offered the possibility of working with a broad range of patients that included treating people with both physical and mental disorders. One of the things that makes occupational therapy unique is it requires understanding not only the patient's disability but who they are as a person. This was a natural fit because I was in the midst of my analysis at the time and learning to understand myself emotionally to transcend the issues in my life that were preventing me from achieving more success. I still remember how happy I was when I was accepted to university, as I expected it to give new meaning and purpose to my life (which it did). It was a very challenging and demanding two year program resulting in a masters degree that allowed me to work with almost any population with a disability from pediatrics to geriatrics.

My first internship was at Bellevue Hospital working with individuals with acute physical disabilities. I felt my supervisor was destructive. Although her role was to provide support and advance my learning she expected me to know everything and picked on my abilities and physical appearance. For example, I recall having a scratch on my arm and she insisted that I had inflicted it upon myself. I had not inflicted it on myself and she had no right to tell me that even if it was the case. Within a few weeks, I realized that she was going to continue to pick on me and not provide any instruction. I discussed this in my analysis and my analyst told me that this was an abusive situation. We discussed how this related to other abusive relationships in my life and I felt encouraged not to submit to sadism. Consequently, I called the advisor of internships at my university to discuss this with her. We came up with a new plan where I would leave the internship and complete it at a later time. Instead, I was asked to spend the remaining time of my internship in a volunteer position at Metropolitan Hospital so I could advance my learning. Although I felt some humiliation for not fulfilling the internship, I was grateful for the understanding of my school advisor and knew it was the right thing to do.

Within the next year, I completed this internship at Rusk Rehabilitation Institute in Manhattan, which was considered the best rehabilitation center in New York City. When I interviewed with the head of the program, she told me that this was not the first time something like this had happened and she was aware of other students who were subject to the same mistreatment. She accepted me into her program and told me I would receive all the support that I needed. It was a wonderful experience and I went from almost flunking to getting an A. I could not have gone from an F to an A without an outside force intervening. This was a lesson to me that I used in working with my students. Too many times parents would tell me that their teacher had it in for their child. This is not unusual but I knew to really investigate to see if it was true. Though I know there could be bias from the parents, I knew from my own experience that a teacher could create an environment that would cause the child to fail. Consequently, I would listen to the teacher's point of view and when I felt that this teacher was singling the child out, I advised the parent accordingly. I remember one lovely student who was being advised to have occupational therapy, physical therapy, psychological therapy, and group therapy despite the fact that I did not think he needed so many services and that too much treatment could be harmful. Too much therapy often causes a child to think "How much is wrong with me?" The mother was afraid if she didn't follow their suggestions exactly, her son would be asked to leave this elite private school. I advised the mother to follow all the school's suggestions but not necessarily the way they said. In this way they would see she was a cooperative parent while still doing what was best for her child. I advised her that they wouldn't ask how frequently he was attending things and that unless she was specifically asked she would not have to reveal it. In other words, I was telling her to do the OT with me and tell them he's also doing the other therapies so that they were appeased. I advised her to only do the other therapies once a month. Fast forward to his following school year, when the child was now in kindergarten and considered one of the outstanding students in class. This was not because I was such a brilliant therapist, it was because I recognized through my analysis that there can be a mismatch between individuals, or students and teachers, and you must figure out the best way to get through it. I no longer view that very painful experience with the abusive supervisor as a terrible thing. It has informed me, as a result of my analysis, that this does happen and I have helped so many parents and children get through it as my analyst helped me.

I discovered in my final internship that pediatrics was home for me. What I learned in my analysis by reviewing my childhood and its impact on my development guided me in my work with children. Although I made every effort not to impose my personal experiences on my students, my analysis truly informed my understanding of how children think and feel, as well as how difficult it is to be the parent of a disabled child. The more I learned about myself in analysis the more psychologically attuned I was with my patients and their parents. Understanding my own disability with low vision as a child informed how I practiced and allowed me to recognize that a child with a disability also impacts their siblings and poses additional challenges to their parents. As I became more experienced, this became an essential and unique approach to the way I worked with children. When I began my analysis I did not consider myself to be a child with a disability, rather I considered myself a person with a deficient personality. This is a common experience for children with invisible disabilities like me. For example, a child with dyslexia, a reading disorder, often felt "stupid" because they had difficulty with reading and writing rather than understanding that they had a learning disability. Their parents also misunderstood and frequently blamed their child for being lazy and not working hard enough. As a result of examining these issues in my analysis, I came to understand that my low vision disability had a parallel impact on me and I was able to use this understanding to help my students and their parents.

The work I did in analysis in understanding how my invisible disability impacted me enabled me to understand my students with more insight. For example, one of my students who I will call Jared, had severe learning disabilities. I worked with him on improving his writing and handwriting. To increase the pace of his progress, I suggested that he work on his handwriting in between sessions. I told him that he would get a pack of Pokemon cards, which he loved, for every page of handwriting that he brought to our next session. The next session he came in and proudly showed me six pages of handwriting. I told him that I was proud of how much he did, but that I felt the quality of what he had produced did not merit six packs of cards. I told him it merited two. Other students took this in stride as they were able to acknowledge that quality was as important as quantity. However, Jared was furious. He ran out of my office into the waiting room and told his mother that I was the worst person in the universe. He wanted to leave immediately and never come back. I instantly understood what was at play. His severe learning disabilities created so much ambiguity in his life that he was more literal than other children. In front of his mother, I explained to them both that it was my fault for not clarifying that the quality of his work was as important as the quantity. I understood his rage because I experienced situations like this as a child myself. My low vision created ambiguity in my life, though for very different reasons. Such ambiguity causes many children anxiety as I learned in understanding myself in analysis. To quell the anxiety that the ambiguity creates, a child makes things black and white in their mind so there is no uncertainty. This happened frequently; many children would try to avoid an activity that they felt they would not succeed at. They also avoided trying new things for the same reason. Once again I understood how to respond to their avoidance because I had used it myself in my childhood. These are examples of how I saw glimpses of myself in my students as a result of having learned why I was either avoidant or enraged in my own childhood due to the limitations my low vision imposed. I had been wise and lucky enough to choose a career that could take my negative experiences as a child and make them meaningful. It allowed me to understand my young students and provide them the help I never got.

CHAPTER 7

Getting Into The Nitty Gritty

As my analysis progressed, I found myself recognizing and at times re-experiencing how painful my childhood had been. In spite of how challenging this was, my analyst encouraged me to persevere because he knew I had the resilience to do so. I discovered that my dissociation and numbness were defense mechanisms to protect myself from the pain. I recall telling my analyst it was as though I had created an invisible shield to protect me. Although my defense mechanisms helped me get through my childhood, they became more and more of a liability as I got older. We were now at the point in my analysis where we could remove that shield to let me experience what I had been through and understand how it affected me. He told me I had already begun to penetrate my defenses and we needed to continue doing that. I said to him "Do you mean I don't need so much armor anymore? That I can handle it?" He replied, "Yes, and remember Penny you're not alone this time and I'm here with you." He helped me recognize that I was ready to fully *feel* and become more alive.

I remember while discussing something very difficult, an aspect of my childhood that I had never dealt with before,I was silent because I was embarrassed of my feelings. My analyst asked me, "What are you thinking?" and after a long silence I told him "I'm thinking I would like to sit on your lap." Of course he did not allow this as that would have been a breach of boundaries. He asked me whose comfort I was seeking and I said "My mothers." This honest admission of my needs and desires was a huge breakthrough. I know we discussed this for the length of the session, however I do not recall it. I speculate that we discussed why I needed so much comfort at this moment as well as what it was like never to have received this kind of comfort from my mother. One thing I am sure of is he also recognized what a breakthrough this was and we explored it further in subsequent sessions until we understood it fully. We were breaking down barriers and in contrast to how I'd felt at the beginning of my analysis, I was able to reveal something I found embarrassing in one session.

It was so difficult to relive those aspects of my childhood that as we unearthed more of it at times I reverted to my defense mechanisms. When first exploring a painful issue it could be overwhelming and consequently the anorexia and bulimarexia intensified. This was self destructive as I was really risking my health by abusing laxatives. It may be hard to believe but the laxative was called *Correctol*! I still remember being in the pharmacy looking at the various kinds of laxatives from which to select. My eye was drawn to the pink box labeled *Correctol*, no doubt because that's what I was hoping it would do. Correct all. (The product was taken off the market several years later because one of its ingredients was found to be damaging to the kidneys. It was even removed from colonoscopy prep for the same reason. I eventually stopped this self-destructive behavior thanks to the intervention of my analyst.) I didn't do this every day. I only did it when it became too difficult to tolerate these painful feelings, usually about once a week. However when I did do it, I made myself very sick. It was a way of controlling the rage I felt at how I was treated when I was young. When I came to a session and my analyst asked me why I looked so sick, I would tell him part of the truth but not the whole truth. I let him believe I had food poisoning or a stomach virus as I told him what my symptoms were. However, he did not think that was the whole truth and asked me more questions. Many years later in my analysis, he told me that he had been very worried about me and that I was behaving masochistically towards myself but unconsciously was behaving sadistically towards him. Once he knew what I really was doing and we discussed it he told me that I really didn't want to do this to myself and that I could stop. When he realized that his interpretations were not sufficient to persuade me to stop, he gave me an ultimatum. I had to stop or he would not treat me anymore. I asked him why, because I had always recovered. He told me it was too dangerous, that I was risking my health, and could accidentally kill myself. He added that I was very treatable but not under these circumstances. He was not going to ignore the elephant in the room, which isn't typical of all analysts. Not every psychoanalyst would've given me that ultimatum. I promised to stop because I was so attached to him and was not willing to lose him. What helped me follow through was a very important interpretation he made. I thought the reason I binged was because I had so restricted my food intake that when I finally succumbed to my hunger I would binge. Then I would purge because I didn't want to gain weight. He told me that he didn't think my motivation was the binging; my motivation was the purging, which represented the purging of my intolerable feelings. I immediately recognized the truth in this and I completely stopped for several months. However, when he took his August vacation I became so sad and depressed that I did take a milder laxative on two occasions. I felt guilty about this and felt I had gone back on my word. I didn't get as sick but I knew I had broken my promise. Having no other outlet for my feelings, I was compelled to purge. It was so important to me that I be honest, that I took the risk of confessing that I had relapsed twice while he was away. He was very understanding and flexible, as he knew how difficult it was for me when he was on his August sabbatical. After that I never abused the laxatives again.

However, that did not end my self destructive behavior. I could not handle the overwhelming feelings of rage I often experienced in our sessions; I needed an outlet. I took it out on myself as opposed to others. My outlet was food. Since I couldn't purge, I started to gain weight. I had been so thin (I weighed 90 lbs at the height of 5 '6 and a half) that it wasn't that difficult to tolerate gaining weight at first. However, as the pounds accumulated I became more depressed which caused the vicious cycle of eating even more and feeling more depressed and out of control. Because food was now my outlet for my angry feelings, I overshot my ideal weight by ten pounds. Imagine how hard it was for a former anorexic to gain 40 lbs. This was horrifying to me, however I no longer had the outlet of purging. During this period of gaining weight, it was a constant subject of my analysis. He listened to me patiently and would reinforce that although this was difficult and I gained more weight than I had wanted, this was far more healthy than where I was previously. He reinforced that I was in a much healthier place and that an extra ten pounds was a small price to pay for my health. When I told him that I felt out of control, he reminded me that I was a person who had more control than most. (Afterall, you need a lot of self control to starve yourself.) With his help I finally got the weight issue under control, lost the extra ten pounds to be my healthy and attractive weight, which I have maintained ever since. I imagine this coincided with my progress in therapy and being less angry. It was now less painful to relive the past.

However, the past was still present. I had just given up anorexia, gotten my relationship with food under control, and was at a healthy and attractive weight for me. At my sister's second wedding, my father told me I needed to lose five more pounds to be more attractive. I was cut to the core and devastated. What a sadistic thing to say. I wish I had responded with "What a horrible thing to say to your recently anorexic daughter!" Instead what I did, as I frequently did in my 20s and 30s, I relied on my sister to help me recover from his sadistic behavior. I had no one else to turn to, not even my mother who had rarely been a source of comfort. My sister often came to my rescue when I was depressed or when I felt mistreated at a family event. I didn't realize it at the time, but it was inappropriate to interfere with the happiness of my sister's wedding day. Although I take responsibility for this, I was used to asking for her comfort because she and my older brother often assumed parental responsibilities. This was unfair to us all. My sister and brother did not have to be asked to do this when my younger brother or I needed help. They filled in the gap that my parents created, despite resenting it at times. They had my back even when I was a pain in theirs. What wonderful siblings I have! My parents had frequently reinforced how important our sibling relationships were. I'm grateful they got this right.

When I returned from the wedding and discussed with my analyst how problematic it had been for me, he agreed that my father's behavior was very sadistic. He was taken aback at how uninformed and cruel his behavior was. This led us to a further discussion of how many times my father was sadistic to me when

I was younger and that my way of dealing with it was masochistic. My siblings and I all internalized some of my father's sadism. I wonder if this was related to a family phenomenon that I refer to as "pass the trash." When my mother upset my sister, my sister would pass that along to my older brother and do something to annoy him. He in turn would pass it along and do something to upset me. I then would do something unkind to my younger brother and make him cry. I referred to this as "pass the trash" because of a poker game we played in our teens with the same name. In the poker game *pass the trash*, you passed your two worst cards to the person on your left making it more difficult for them to win. As the youngest, Ricky had no one to pass the trash to.

Although they were absent too much, I do have many fond memories of my parents. My mother, who made my eye doctor appointments, orchestrated it so my father and I went at the same time on a Saturday as we were both due for a check up. This was unusual because my mother usually took me to the eye doctor on a weekday. What was also unusual was that I was very nervous about this arrangement, as I had never been alone with my father and I was afraid I wouldn't be able to converse or relate to him without the buffer of my siblings. Before our appointment, he took me to lunch at a nearby coffee shop. As it turns out we easily conversed, especially because I discovered my father could be very charming. That day I had my first cheeseburger but not my last. I remember a very popular song at the time was playing on the jukebox. The song was *Volare*, a love song sung by Dean Martin. Then we went to the eye doctor and we were told that the doctor was running quite late, so my father suggested that we go across the street to the Metropolitan Museum of Art and return when they told us the doctor would be ready for us. (My mother never would have done this.) At the end of that afternoon, I think I had fallen in love with my father. (I had repressed my Oedipal phase which was confirmed by a psychological evaluation I had when I was 26. This will be elaborated on in greater depth in Chapter 12.) I remember equally special times with my mother. Shopping, dining in restaurants, and traveling with my siblings. One of my fondest memories was her taking me to the Broadway play *The Miracle Worker* when I was 11 years old. The play is about Hellen Keller and Annie Sullivan. She took only me because of my experience with a visual disability, demonstrating her empathy for my low vision. One of the most exceptional and loving ways she demonstrated her empathy for me was that starting when I was eight years old, at every visit to my eye doctor my mother asked him if I could get contact lenses. He said I was too young but she persisted at every visit until he reluctantly agreed when I was almost 12. In addition, she had herself fitted for contact lenses so she would know what the experience would be like for me when I finally got mine. She learned how difficult it could be to insert and remove them and how easy it was to lose one as they were so small. A month after I got my contact lenses, I did lose one and because they were so expensive I was afraid my parents would be angry at me. My mother's experience taught her how difficult it was to handle them and how easy it was to lose them. With no reproach, she ordered a new one for me. Contact lenses changed my life. Not only did it improve my physical appearance, which was important to a 12 year old, but most importantly I was now able to see 20/40.

Although I remember well when my parents were involved with us, for example attending mother's day or father's day at my school, visiting day at camp, etc, these examples are what most parents would consider ordinary but mine considered exceptional. Throughout my childhood they often said quality time was more important than quantity time. However, they took this to an extreme and they were absent more than they were present. I have come to believe that children prefer quantity time with quality of relationship. For example, a child might enjoy accompanying their mother to the grocery store just to be with her, as opposed to not being with her at all. Most parents would not consider attending their child's play at school, attending piano recitals, visiting them at camp, or attending their high school graduation to be "quality time."

When I first discussed my parenting in my analysis, my analyst brought to my attention that I would come in one session and describe how remote they were, how absent they were, and how neglected we all were. The next session I would come in and describe the times when they treated me in a caring fashion. He told me it was as if I was taking back what I had said in the previous session. I used to feel that the good things they did canceled out the bad when in fact, what I learned in analysis is that they coexist rather than cancel each other out. I still recognize that they coexist, so I wanted to write the good to provide a fair account for the reader.

CHAPTER 8

———

Nitty Gritty Part 2

As my analysis progressed, the relationship between me and my analyst was examined in more depth. He felt I was ready to explore and take more responsibility for my behavior and that was best accomplished by examining how I related to him. This is a unique feature of psychoanalysis. A core tenet of psychoanalysis is that what happens in relationships outside the office is replicated with the analyst within the office. A useful aspect of this process is the examination of both transference and countertransference. Transference is the phenomenon that repeatedly occurs in analysis when the patient doesn't see the therapist in the present day but projects feelings from past relationships onto him. In my case, I would often feel my analyst was criticizing me in response to something I said because I was projecting feelings onto him from my critical parents.

As I've mentioned, I often would get angry because I felt he was being critical and judgemental just as my parents were. He would explain that this was a projection on my part and that he wasn't being critical. I did not accept this easily because the painful feelings that were elicited by my feeling criticized made me so angry. I would often adamantly disagree with him and tell him that he *was* being critical. For example, I often mistook his asking me a question as criticism. I felt I was being undermined. In fact, I would eventually learn he simply wanted to know more and was truly asking a question without judgment. For example, he might ask me a question like "Why did you feel that way?" but I heard "You shouldn't have felt that way."

Countertransference is the analyst engaging in a similar process where he projects his feelings onto his patient. When this occurs, he has been trained to examine what is triggering his own feelings, whether positive or negative, that causes this projection. His awareness of what is at play in his own countertransference is then used to help the patient. Examining transference and countertransference is an essential feature of psychoanalysis. I can only speak from my point of view but examining and accepting one's projections was often very difficult. I would get overly angry and insist that he was being critical and he would point out that he wasn't, it was just a comment or a question. At times he might ask me why I had responded to someone the way I did, but I would hear *you shouldn't have responded that way.* This happened frequently and as I've mentioned I mistook his probing as criticism. I would argue stubbornly and vociferously and insist that he was wrong. There were times when I was so angry that this anger would persist for several sessions. Eventually, I found it so unpleasant to argue session after session that I would come in and tell him "Okay, now I get it and you're right." What I didn't tell him at the time was that I hadn't changed my mind and I still thought he was wrong, but I just wanted to move on to something else. This actually represented progress because I was no longer the meek and submissive patient I was when we began. Eventually within a month or two, I would come to understand what he was trying to help me realize. Sometimes I wondered how he was able to put up with me because I could barely put up with myself.

Another time I came into my session and told my analyst how angry I was at a friend for canceling our dinner plans at the last minute. She claimed she was sick but did not seem sick to me. I didn't believe her and felt she was either accepting a better invitation that night or was dismissing me. Either way, I experienced this as hurtful. He would ask why I didn't believe her and I told him that it was because it was so last minute that if she truly was sick she would've told me earlier. He asked me why I couldn't give my friend the benefit of the doubt. I told him it was because my parents disappointed me at the last minute all the time. I thought he was taking her side over mine and was reluctant to give up my point of view. As I mentioned, I would be angry at him for many sessions until I couldn't take it anymore and finally pretended to agree with him so we could move on. The same issue came up multiple times until I could change my way of understanding other people's behavior. In this example I came to learn that I didn't know what was at play with my friend and there was no way for me to know whether she was telling the truth or not. It wasn't fair to assume the worst.

As I mentioned before, it was hard for me to accept being mistaken because it made me feel blind and caused me to doubt everything. I had very black and white ways of viewing relationships and I held onto those beliefs so tightly that it was difficult to let them go. I'm not sure if I can help the reader understand how incredibly difficult this was and how enraged I often was when I left his office. It elicited self destructive feelings though I did not act on them. I no longer abused laxatives and I did not use drugs or alcohol. At one point l asked my analyst why he thought I didn't turn to drugs and alcohol when I was so angry. He said "What do you think?", a common question throughout my analysis. On reflection, I said "I think I didn't do it because using drugs and alcohol would have given me too much pleasure and not been punishing enough." (It was a good thing that I did not go down that path as I might've ended up with a drug or alcohol addiction. So there was at least one silver lining in my being so masochistic!) One way I soothed myself was by expressing my feelings in poems that were often related to dreams I had had. I felt poetry would capture my unconscious feelings better than prose. Below are two poems that reflect both positive and painful aspects of my analysis, which were inspired by dreams. Re-reading them 44 years later, I realized I relied on writing poems to express my feelings. I think these poems truly capture what it was like being in analysis.

I also came up with a very safe, although unusual way of calming myself. I would stroke my arm with the tines of a fork, which didn't even leave scratch marks because I applied so little pressure. It was so soothing that within about five minutes my equilibrium was restored.

As time went on it became easier to relinquish my black and white point of view and I started to understand that relationships have nuance. By using our relationship, he helped me understand other people's points of view, not only my own. He did this through his insistence that he had his own point of view as I had mine. It was a slow process because I could be so stubborn. One of the reasons my analysis took so long was because I spent so much time insisting on my own point of view. Ultimately I learned that it was natural for people to have differing perspectives and it became easier for me to consider what theirs might be. I no longer live in that black and white world. I no longer believe that if I'm wrong it means I'm blind. No matter how long it took me to arrive at this destination, it was priceless.

The Three Eyed Monster

I

I talk about the present
And you bring up my past
We both work toward the future
But will my courage last
To face the three eyed monster
Despite the fear and pain
To brave despair and darkness
In order to be sane.

I enter into battle
Without my armor on
While you stand there observing
The war that rages on.
Though wounded I continue
To flail and fight the foe
But then you have to leave and
Inflict the final blow.

You've joined the three eyed monster
It seems as my wounds bleed

And as tears stream down my face
I'm all consumed by need.
I cannot see the monster
Now blinded by my pain.
Perhaps when not alone here
I'll face it once again.

II

Last night the three eyed monster
Wove riddles through my dream.
With images and visions
Revealed to me the seem.
A past and present bonded
By memories of my youth
Forming patterns of future
Designed with threads of truth.

The monster was my ally
Whispering not to fear
Materials before me
Which would help us to clear
The secrets that were buried
Underlayers of debris
Made by well intentioned

Persons who could not see

That monsters once were fairies
And myths are not the facts
That feelings are a part of us
They are the secret pact
Turning monsters and fairies
Into mere human beings
Expressing the inner soul
That each one of us sings.

The monster is my friend now
Its three eyes are my own
With past present and future
No, I am not alone.
With it as my companion
And with you as my guide
We all move toward the future
With eyes now opened wide.

4/27-5/2/79

CHAPTER 9

Charlie Brown, Lucy, and the Football

Sadomasochism is part of human nature though there is disagreement among therapists and psychoanalysts about its definition and manifestations. Although it is universal, the degree of sadomasochism in individuals varies considerably. A very mild form of its universal expression is that comedy and humor often revolve around sadomasochistic circumstances. I cannot think of a better example than the relationship of the Peanuts characters Charlie Brown and Lucy. Lucy continually baits Charlie Brown by convincing him he should trust her. Experience has taught him that she is not trustworthy, nevertheless he cannot resist her persuasiveness and always gets tricked by her removing the football. One of the many reasons the Peanuts comic strip is still popular after 73 years and despite the passing of its creator is its sadomasochism. Charles Schulz, the creator of Peanuts, was famously quoted, "You can't create humor out of happiness."[3] This is an excellent example of how sadomasochism works in comedy. Reading a fictional comic

---

3 Charles Schulz, Charlie Brown Snoopy and Me, Doubleday 1980

strip is very different from actually being in a sadomasochistic relationship. A favorite example of mine was the Saturday Night Live (SNL) cartoon, the *Mr. Bill Show*. Clearly I wasn't the only one who enjoyed this because it was a part of almost every episode for the first six seasons of SNL. The *Mr. Bill Show* featured a similar dynamic as the one Charlie Brown and Lucy had between its two main characters Mr. Bill and Sluggo. Mr. Bill would tease and bait him, Sluggo would do his best to resist taking the bait. However, Mr. Bill would sound so sincere that he wasn't going to trick him again that Sluggo always took the bait. (Probably one of the reasons he was called Sluggo.) I really don't remember why or how this came up in my analysis, however my analyst used it to help me understand sadomasochism in relationships.

Another prime example of the use of sadomasochistic relationships in comedy is between Jerry and Newman in the hit television series *Seinfeld*. In fact, many if not most of the relationships in *Seinfeld* have an overt sadomasochistic element. This is very pervasive in comedy. One of the reasons we laugh is because we vicariously enjoy the meanness we often feel towards others but are taught not to express. However, when it is real and operating in marital relationships, friendships, or familial relationships it's not so funny to be treated sadistically. This was a theme in my analysis that we discussed often to improve my relationships. We discussed how sadomasochism was an aspect of many of my relationships. Part of analysis is going over the same issue in different contexts.

Understanding how sadomasochism was affecting my life surfaced repeatedly in many different ways.

Medical procedures are often experienced by children as sadistic, especially if they are not told the truth about them. I remember hating getting a shot of any kind well into young adulthood. The reason I viewed this as sadistic was I was always told that the shot wouldn't hurt and yet the shot always hurt. I always experienced this as a lie. Lying can be a form of sadism. I think the first time it came up in my analysis was when I was discussing my experience as a toddler undergoing painful eye examinations. In exploring how my very poor vision affected me, we discussed how the medical treatments were experienced by me as sadistic despite them being medically necessary. My reaction to the insertion of eyedrops, bright lights being shown into my eyes, and having my eyes patched for two years was to resist. I often had to be pinned down and restrained because I was trying so hard to evade these procedures. No one was providing comfort or explaining in a soothing voice why these procedures were necessary and that it would be over relatively quickly. Following the insertion of the drops, my mother and I were sent to the waiting room until they took effect, usually 20–30 minutes. I was only 2 or 3 years old and had little to distract or entertain me. Had I had a mother who was capable of sitting me in her lap, hugging me, and soothing me with stories, it would have been significantly less traumatic. When I returned to the doctor, bright lights were shown in my eyes to examine my retinas, which was very painful. It was difficult for me to cooperate with this procedure and my resistance could be viewed as sadism on my part because it made it more difficult for the doctor to examine me. In addition, neither my mother nor the doctor understood why I was so uncooperative, which added to their sadism because they made me feel like a "bad girl" for not being submissive.

It is commonly accepted that sadomasochistic relationships begin in infancy as no child gets all their needs met in a timely fashion. Since they don't have language to tell their parents what they need they experience a certain amount of frustration and deprivation. This is likely to be experienced as cruelty, as unintended as it is. The parent on the other hand feels helpless in soothing their child so a sadomasochistic feature inadvertently is introduced into the relationship from the very beginning. However, the degree to which an individual engages in sadomasochism depends on other factors in their development. I want to emphasize there are many factors that make this a greater or lesser feature of someone's personality and character. Trauma or other adverse experiences in childhood will impact an individual's tendency towards engaging in sado-masochistic relationships. For some individuals, the extent of their involvement in sadomasochism is limited to the pleasure they get by experiencing it in comedy. For children who experience trauma or other adverse events in childhood there may be more attraction to sadomasochistic relationships. The severity of those adverse experiences may translate into a personality that features sadomasochism as an embedded character trait.

My adverse experience with low vision and the medical procedures associated with it primed me for being drawn to involvement in sadomasochism. Additionally, my father was too often sadistic towards me. I distinctly recall my analyst pointing out that my father was being sadistic when he asked me how many fingers he was holding up after every eye doctor visit. A day that was already difficult for me, he made worse. I didn't agree with my analyst at first, probably because I was so accustomed to it. Some people might not realize how that is being sadistic because my father might have just been interested in how well I saw. However after discussing this in analysis, I realized if my father wanted to know how well I saw, all he had to do was ask my mother or my doctor. Instead, unconsciously, I chose a sadistic way that emphasized to me my inadequacies. Today when the eye doctor tries to measure my vision, I cannot read the eye chart so he holds his fingers up, as my dad did to determine whether my acuity has changed. This is not sadistic because it is the only way to measure any changes in my vision. My vision is so poor in my left eye that I cannot see how many fingers there are even when his fingers are as close to my eye as possible. I've adapted so well to my vision loss that I find this is funny and laugh. I think to myself, *why are you even bothering to try to measure my vision?* …unless he were to use one of those foam fingers they hold up at hockey games. I'm laughing as I write this. I turned my father's sadism into a humorous interaction that makes me feel positive rather than negative about myself. (The personal assistant I am dictating this to is laughing with me. I did bring the foam finger in, everyone laughed, and I had a sense of humor that I couldn't even see that.)

Later in my analysis when I was more aware of my father's sadistic tendencies, I recognized that from time to time he was drawing me into a sadomasochistic situation like the one with Lucy and Charlie Brown. I recall when I was thinking about a career change he offered me a position in the family business, flattering me with what an asset I would be to the company. I resisted taking what I thought was bait, but he persisted in enticing me to consider this by telling me how talented I was and how much I had to offer the company and other similar kinds of flattery. I tried to resist taking the bait and said "No dad it's not really my interest, it's not such a good fit." but he insisted and increased his flattery, ultimately telling me what a huge salary I would make. At that point I finally took the bait and told him I'd *consider* it. As soon as I gave in, he smiled with glee and said "I was only joking. I never thought you'd be any good in the family business." He finally got what he had always wanted from this interaction: my humiliation.

Despite discussing this in one of my analytic sessions and fully understanding what my father was doing, I was still drawn to sado-masochistic relationships especially with men. Another example is my father's brother, my uncle Dick. He was even more sadistic than my father. He repeatedly was the Lucy to my Charlie Brown. I remember a family dinner on vacation in August, when he baited me by asking me if I was sleeping with my analyst. I was far enough along in my analysis at that point that I had learned the only way to deal with sadists is to disengage and not respond to their sadism. I told him "That's a horrible thing to ask me and I will not dignify your question with an answer." Since I didn't take the bait, he then turned toward my seven year old niece who had recently been adopted from Guatemala by my brother and his wife. He told her that she was not a true Mishkin because she was adopted and that she should make sure to retain her native language of Spanish. In the past, I was the one who was brought to tears but since I no longer would engage with him he brought an innocent young child to tears, who told me the next day she wasn't a true Mishkin.

As an aside, when I discussed this event the first session after vacation I told my analyst that my uncle had said something horrible to me but I didn't take the bait. He asked me what he had said but I couldn't remember what it was. An excellent example of repression. I did recall that it had something to do with my relationship with him but that was as much as I could remember. I was so curious to learn what he had actually said that I called my sister who witnessed it. She was incredulous and exclaimed "What? You don't remember what he said to you? It was so awful!" Once she told me, I remembered it all.

As I mentioned in Chapter 7, my masochism was often expressed in the way I made myself sick by abusing laxatives. As we discussed later in my analysis, I was not only being masochistic to myself. Unconsciously, I was being sadistic to my analyst because of how much I caused him to worry about me. I think he gave me the ultimatum to stop, not only for my benefit but also because he wouldn't allow me to be sadistic to him. From his perspective, I was unconsciously treating him sadistically because he worried about me and felt responsible for my well being.

Another important feature of my attraction to sadomasochism was my perceiving myself as a victim and living in victimhood; a form of self pity. We discussed that I was a victim because of my parent's limitations, my poor vision, and because I was raped. But I was choosing to live in victimhood and re-experience my victimization too frequently. We discussed that everyone suffers at some point in their life, as it is part of being human, however living in victimhood is a choice. Choosing victimhood, which meant I was choosing misery over happiness, was another form of my masochism. This was a concept that was difficult for me to grasp at first because I did not make the distinction between being a victim and living in victimhood. Being a victim was the result of sadism, choosing to live in victimhood was masochism. Once I fully understood this it was extraordinarily liberating. Understanding that I could *choose happy* was something I had never considered before. Once I understood that I had the ability to *choose happy* and discard victimhood, it was transformational. It is a perspective that allows me to have a wonderful life even though I am now blind. Although my life is very different than it was three years ago, my life is just as wonderful as it had been. Understanding this has allowed me to accept the detour my poor vision has created. My joy, satisfaction, and gratification now come from other things but they are just as deeply rewarding and intensely satisfying as before.

CHAPTER 10

—————

Violation

My first experience with violation was the necessary medical procedures performed on my eyes beginning at age two. When I had to wear the eye patch between the ages of three and five, I struggled against its application by my nanny as most children do. I consider this a violation because I was saying no, but no didn't mean no. My nanny was very strict and insisted that I submit. Had it been done with understanding and kindness and without the threat of being punished if I didn't cooperate, it might not have felt like a violation. As it turns out, it was completely unnecessary. There was absolutely no medical evidence that this was going to help me and it did not. What it did was adversely impact my development because I became more shy and introverted and less trusting of adults and doctors, *and likely set me up for future violation*. This was a very early lesson in submission. A few years later my nanny asked me if I knew what the word "heed" meant. I said no and she proceeded to tell me "Heed means you submit. Heed means you do whatever I tell you to do." And I was threatened and occasionally punished.

Another factor that led to violation was that my low vision did not allow me to trust my own perceptions. Consequently, I was very gullible and easily tricked which led to negative experiences and also primed me for attraction to sadomasochistic experiences. When I was 22 years old and in graduate school in Boston I did what almost every college student in Boston did. I put my thumb out and hitch hiked. I was always in a hurry to get places and either took the trolley or hitch hiked, whichever opportunity came first. One evening in March I left my class and waited for the trolley when a car pulled over offering me a ride. I had what I call the "uh-oh" feeling, which told me not to get into the car but I ignored that feeling because I didn't trust my perceptions. The two men in the car were both black and I will never forget saying to myself, "Penny, don't be a racist." The color of their skin should not have made any difference to me, I should never have gotten into a car with two men which allowed for me to be trapped. This shows how poor my judgment was and how I couldn't trust my instincts. I told them my destination and when they veered off the route to my home, I innocently exclaimed "Oh, you're going the wrong way!" It should have been my first inkling that something was not right but I was so naive that I just thought they made a mistake. A few minutes later when they stopped before an unfamiliar house, I knew I was in trouble. The driver got out of the car to urinate, which I saw as an opportunity to escape. He punched me in the face, split my lip, and shoved me back in the car. I started to bargain, offering him all the money I had with me, which wasn't that much. I told them I came from a wealthy family and I would give him my father's phone number because he would pay a substantial amount for my freedom. This made no difference. They refused the offer which might have given me another opportunity to escape. Once the driver was back in the car, the other got in the back seat with me. They got on a highway to conceal what they were planning, which was taking turns raping me in the back seat. The first rapist removed only my boots and underwear because I was wearing a skirt. He penetrated me but was unable to maintain an erection and could not complete the intercourse. The driver made fun of him and seemed to me like a bully, as he mocked his friend's impotence. The first rapist was the weaker of the two. To my surprise, it made me feel a little sorry for him. He kept trying until his friend barked at him, "Since you can't get the job done, it's now my turn." Then they pulled over to the shoulder of the highway and traded places.

He had no trouble getting the job done. I was still a virgin so this was very painful. When he was inside me, he insisted that I repeat over and over that I was cumming and that I was enjoying it. Having to pretend that I was getting pleasure from being raped was almost worse than the forced intercourse itself. It was many many years before I could ever utter the words "I'm coming." He then forced his penis into my mouth and held my head down so I could not withdraw. This allowed him to get hard again. He then penetrated me again and as before made me pretend I was enjoying it and that I was cumming. This happened at least three times. Throughout the whole experience, I wondered how it would end. I thought it could end with them killing me because they had threatened me with a knife, but more frequently imagined it would end with them leaving me on the side of the highway completely naked. They never completely removed all my clothes, so I'm not sure why this image came to mind other than it would put me in the most exposed, vulnerable, and humiliating position. Which would have been consistent with their cruelty.

Earlier when I had offered all my money to the driver, some change fell out of my wallet. I surreptitiously kept trying to find the coins and finally found a dime. I soothed myself by imagining that I would be able to find a payphone, which in those days cost exactly one dime, so I could call the police and summon help. I clutched this dime throughout the entire experience as I felt it was the only hope of survival. At the beginning, they tried to make me drink liquor. I knew how to submit and I told them I would take pot or a drug because it wouldn't make me vomit, just not alcohol. I knew the alcohol would make me sick and I worried if I vomited they might have another reason to kill me. They were not offering me a nice bottle of cabernet, but hard spirits such as scotch or whiskey and I knew I would not be able to keep those down. I did persuade them and did not have to drink the alcohol. My analyst asked me why I thought they would kill me if

I vomited and I told him I felt if I made them angry by vomiting in their car it would give them an additional reason to do it. It echoed the threat of punishment and spanking by my nanny if I did not submit.

One of the worst aspects of the rape was that I knew exactly how to submit and that the *rape felt familiar.* Submit or something bad will happen to you. On the one hand my submission may have saved my life, on the other hand, how horrible is it to be raped and feel that it is familiar. My analyst and I discussed the role of submission in my life repeatedly. It didn't exist just in my rape nor did it simply exist with my nanny. Submission was ingrained in my personality. As a child I was always a follower and I did what I was told. Until my analysis, in my relationships I was almost always the follower. What I kept to myself at times was how angry I was because it was so one sided. However, this was my choice.)

As I've mentioned, we were on the highway and the first rapist who was now driving saw a patrol car in his rearview mirror. The other rapist, who was still making me suck his penis, cautioned the driver not to speed up so they would not capture the attention of the patrol car who was most likely routinely looking for anyone breaking traffic laws. Nevertheless, the driver panicked and sped up. A chase now ensued. Now both men panicked and my head was released. I was so relieved that this at least four hour ordeal was over one way or another, whether we would crash or they would be caught. At point I didn't care if I ended up injured or dead,

I was just relieved that it was over. While they were exiting the highway, they tried to leave the car while it was moving, leaving me in it. Fortunately the car crashed into a fence before they could do that. They exited and fled across a snow covered field. The policeman had no idea what he had just encountered. I got out of the car and ran barefoot into this big, strongly built policeman's arms as I cried and told him what happened. He called for backup which arrived quickly. I was put in a police car and taken to a gynecologist so he could examine me and gather evidence. The gynecologist was especially kind and gentle. I felt he knew how difficult it was to be examined after what I had just been through. I knew how important it was for the police to collect as much evidence as possible so despite the additional trauma of this examination, I knew it was necessary. I was then driven to the police station which was in Worcester Massachusetts, approximately an hour from Boston. They took my statement of what had happened. The rapists were caught quickly because they had left footprints over the snow. I was asked to identify them in the police station. Seeing them elicited all the fear I had had of being their captive. I cowered in the corner as far away as possible from the two-way mirror. After I identified them, I called my roommate to let her know what had happened. She knew something was wrong because it was now midnight and on a weeknight my routine was to be back at our apartment by eight o clock. She and two friends of hers who lived in our building drove to Worcester to pick me up. I asked her to bring me a change of clothes, as the police kept what I had been wearing as evidence. I then called my father. Throughout my life my father had told me he would be there if I really needed him. I believed him. He was semi-retired and spent four days in New York for business then ten days at his home in Florida. When my father was in New York he stayed with my brother. When I called, my 24 year old brother answered the phone and I told him "Joe, just put dad on the phone." Then I blurted out to my father that I had just been raped. He asked me if I was okay. Since I had been trained all my life to always be okay and deny my feelings, I automatically said yes. What he should have asked was "Are you safe?" Now sitting in the police station, I *was* safe. But I was not okay. My roommate arrived and took me home. I got home at around three in the morning and shortly after my mother called. Our conversation was brief because of the late hour. She told me to call her the next day so we could speak at greater length. I then took a longer than usual shower, probably at least an hour. At that point, I noticed the bottom of my foot was very deeply cut. I think that shows how numb and in shock I was that I didn't feel the pain of how badly cut my foot was until then. I had been walking around on that foot for at least four hours and did not feel it or have any pain. By the time I got into bed it must have been 4:30 or 5:00 in the morning. Of course I was very sad, but what really surprised me was that after being touched in a way that I did not seek and that was repulsive, I so wanted to be held.

It felt so empty being alone in my bed and I was surprised at how much I craved the comfort of being held. In my analysis, I came to understand that my denial of longing for my parent's comfort was broken through by such a horrific experience.

The next day two detectives, a man and a woman, came to my apartment to interview me. We went over my statement from the night before and I was asked further questions. I was very lucky in that they were so kind, gentle, and thoughtful during this interview. (It is also astonishing that there was a policewoman there in 1972. Imagine how few women were even on the police force.) Her presence, as well as the kindness of the male detective, were very comforting. After the interview, I called my mother as she requested and our housekeeper answered the phone. When she told my mother that it was me, my mother told her she would call me back when her bridge game was finished a few hours later. In contrast to the kindness of the policemen, my mother brushed me off as though I didn't matter. In addition, my father matched her lack of caring. That Friday morning he got on a plane as he originally planned to go back to Florida. He easily could have, and I do believe should have, changed his plans and gotten on a plane to Boston.

Next I called the psychiatrist I was seeing at the time to let him know what happened and to schedule an appointment, which was the next day Saturday. I still remember what I was wearing that day. I wore the clothing that would make me look the most innocent and pure for no one else but myself. I told him what had happened in great detail. I am not sure why he asked me this question nor did I think it was appropriate, but he asked me if I got any pleasure from being raped. I was stunned, said no, and explained that it was very painful both physically and emotionally. I'm not sure why I ever went back to him but there were no rape crisis centers then and because I was in crisis it would have been hard to find another professional in a timely fashion. At first I thought he was getting excited by the description of what I had gone through. Especially because of the question he asked, wanting to know if I had climaxed. I feel very strongly that he never should have asked me this, at least not so soon. In contrast, I know my analyst never would have asked me such a question. He would have waited for me to tell him if I felt guilty about my body feeling sexual pleasure, *if* that had been the case. I did not feel pleasure but some women do and they feel shame about those feelings, though they shouldn't. Years later, after watching many seasons of Law and Order: SVU, I learned that some women *do* climax despite the horrific circumstances. Their body just responds that way and it is not under their control; similar to how we respond to being tickled. We may not invite it, we may not like it, yet we laugh anyway. It doesn't mean that it was enjoyable or pleasurable.

Unknown to me, I was at a higher risk of being raped than many other women. 1 in 4 girls are sexually abused in childhood before the age of 18. According to the CDC[4], "The percentage of women who were raped as children or adolescents and also raped as adults was more than two times higher than the percentage among women without an early rape history." In other words, young girls who are sexually assaulted are twice as likely to be revictimized as adults. Disabled women are at an even greater risk for sexual assault and revictimization. I do not have a specific memory of childhood sexual abuse, but during my analysis we discussed the possibility of it because of a series of recurring dreams where I was sexually abused. I have never told anybody in my family because it is not a clear and distinct memory. However, I did have a suspect but not enough information to ever speak of it or make any specific accusations. My dreams always featured my uncle, the one who asked me if I had slept with my shrink. He was often verbally sexually inappropriate to me. The dreams were nightmares, very vivid, and very disturbing. I do remember very clearly that when I was between the ages of 8 and 10 that he had the opportunity. My uncle and my father were in business together. The business was located in Pennsylvania where my uncle lived and they took turns conducting business with my uncle sometimes coming to New York and my father sometimes going to Pennsylvania. There were several times when my uncle was in New York and missed the

---

4 "Fast Facts: Preventing Sexual Violence | violence Prevention | injury Center | CDC," Centers for Disease Control and Prevention, June 22, 2022, https://www.cdc.gov/violenceprevention/ sexualviolence/fastfact.html.

last train back to his home. When this happened my uncle would stay at our apartment. My bedroom had one bed, but my sister's bedroom had two double beds. Consequently, my uncle was given my bedroom and I was carried by him in the middle of the night to the second bed in my sister's room. I do remember waking up when I was carried and knowing it was my uncle taking me from one room to the other. He certainly had the opportunity to take advantage of the situation. However, I don't remember anything specific. I would wake up disoriented and blind because my glasses were still under the pillow where I had fallen asleep. I found it very upsetting to wake up in my sister's room and I asked my mother *why*. She explained it to me, so the next several times he moved me from my bed I knew what had happened. However, I never liked it or got used to it and it was always disturbing. Regardless, he should never have been the one to carry me, it should have been my father. A better solution would have been for him to sleep on one of the long couches in the living room, which had a bathroom nearby. Although childhood sexual abuse was hardly thought of at the time, this is consistent with my parent's inability to consider what this would mean to me and protect me.

When I started having these nightmares my analyst suggested that they might be memories of sexual abuse in childhood. I had a very difficult time accepting that this is what the dreams meant. He told me I ticked off all the boxes for someone with a history of childhood sexual assault. Remember, 1 in 4 girls are sexually abused in childhood before the age of 18. In addition, children with disabilities are three times more likely to be sexually abused than non disabled children. Sexually abused children are also more likely to be sexually abused again in adulthood, as was the case for me. For these reasons, my analyst told me I checked off almost all the boxes for someone who was sexually abused in childhood. I was afraid and had difficulty having healthy relationships with men. I was anorexic and self destructive. I had depression and anxiety and recurring nightmares about abuse. I experienced disturbances of sexual desire and arousal. I specifically remember not recognizing feelings of sexual arousal well before the rape. When I was 11 and in summer camp I was having trouble falling asleep and felt wetness and "funny feelings" in my vagina. I thought it meant I was getting my period for the first time. I went to the bathroom, discovered that I did not have my period, but thought this was indication that it was imminent. I did not want to get my period until I was 12 because I thought it was abnormal to get it sooner. I took my washcloth and ran it under water to make it as hot as possible. I pressed it against my vagina in the hope that it would stop me from getting my period. It wasn't until I was 20 that I recognized that those "funny feelings" were an indication that I was sexually aroused. If I was sexually abused as a child, it would explain why I was so numb to sexual desire. Although I had nightmares about my uncle, it's possible that it was a screen memory, which is a defense against recalling a *too* painful memory. It's also possible that it was my nanny's boyfriend because when he was over they drank beer and would get tipsy. I have always hated the smell and taste of beer.

Three days after my rape my roommate asked me "Where are your parents?" She was shocked that my parents had not come to be with me. Although I find this unbelievable today, prior to that question I didn't realize they weren't there because I didn't miss them and was so used to them being absent. I felt their behavior indicated they didn't love me or care enough to be with me. I'm not sure how comforting their presence would have been, as this was far from a strength of theirs. Indeed I have a feeling I would've had to comfort them more than they comforted me. (Remember I always had to be okay.) I was enraged when I finally recognized that they didn't care enough about me to even come give me a hug. I found this incomprehensible however, for the first time in my life I realized there was really something wrong with my parents as opposed to there being something wrong with me. About six months later, I asked my older brother why no one showed up for me. He told me, and I absolutely knew it was the truth, that after I got off the phone with my father from the police station and he told my brother what happened, my brother said "Dad lets get in the car and drive to Boston to be with Penny." My father said it wasn't necessary because I had told him I was okay. (Really? You're daughter has just been brutally raped by two men and almost murdered and she's fine?) My father persuaded my brother not to

come. He convinced everyone that I was fine. My father's attitude dictated everyone's behavior. I'm pretty sure if the roles were
reversed and my sister had been raped, I think my father would have
convinced me not to go comfort her either. There was enormous
power to my father's indifference.

Three weeks later was Passover and I had originally planned
to come home for this holiday. For the first time in my life, I did
not want to be with my family because I felt so mistreated and
so unloved. However, my roommate went to her home for the
holiday as did my other friends. I thought it would be worse to be
all alone only three weeks after the rape, so I chose to go to New
York. My mother told me that the only room they had for me in
the apartment was the living room couch. To me it felt like it just
went from bad to worse to unimaginable. This was unacceptable
to me because I would have no privacy and only offering the couch
once again made me feel I had no importance to them. I chose to
stay at a hotel, which I paid for, that was near the apartment. By
this point, I was not only sad and hurt but furious that they didn't
seem to care what I had just been through. I felt the message they
were sending me was that it didn't matter if I was alive or if I was
dead. This was incredibly painful. The first time I saw them in
New York, I told them there was something we had to discuss. For
the first time in my life I confronted them. I remember standing
in the living room with them seated on the couch. It felt like they
were students in my principal's office. I told them I simply could

not understand why they were treating me this way. I enumerated their failures: the fact that my father went to Florida, that he talked my brother out of coming to be with me, that my mother would not take my phone call because she was playing bridge, and that all they had to offer me to sleep on was the living room couch. I told them, "I simply cannot understand your behavior. I almost died that night and I cannot comprehend why you didn't want to see me, or touch me, or hug me. How could you treat your daughter with such indifference? Do I really not matter to you at all?"

When I related this to my analyst, I quoted the opening scene of Shakespeare's *Macbeth*, "Fair is foul and foul is fair." I frequently referred to this line when discussing the way my parents treated me. Their response was that they didn't understand their behavior either. I think they truly believed that they would be there if I ever needed them, despite the fact that they never attended to a sick child. I don't think they ever expected to be tested the way my rape tested them. They said they would never forgive themselves for behaving that way. However, they had many opportunities to behave differently going forward. When I testified before the grand jury in May, my mother wasn't there, my father wasn't there. They sent my 24 year old brother. How unfair and uncaring to my brother to have to take care of his sister, how unloving to the both of us. He did as well as he could to provide comfort. There was another opportunity for them to demonstrate that they were sorry for how they behaved and that they did in fact love me. When

I testified at the rape trial itself in late June in Worcester, Massachusetts, someone had to drive me there. I felt grateful that they didn't just hire a driver. My mother drove me to the trial, however my father went to work that day as though nothing unusual was happening. How unloving he was to my mother. He should have been there to support her as well as me. I was grateful that my mother was there, however she would not come into the courtroom when I testified. Once again I had no support or comfort. Fortunately, I had the strength to proceed without her. The rapists' family was there but not mine. My mother told me it would be too painful to listen to my testimony. I thought to myself, *If you think it's painful to listen to what happened to me, imagine what it was like to live through it? How can you be so limited that you cannot put my needs before yours?* This was the story of my life. I didn't say it to her because I was so grateful that she had just driven me there. This was so typical of the way they had always treated their children. My siblings and I all had to find our own strength or get strength from one another to survive their indifference. My older brother and sister recognized at an early age that they would never get all they needed from our parents. They went out of their way to develop relationships with teachers and camp counselors to provide what our parents did not. I did not know how to create that kind of connection. I appreciated whatever was offered to me as I was used to getting so little. On the drive home, we stopped for dinner and I felt the need to express my gratitude to my mother by offering to pay for our dinner. She accepted. I took her acceptance of my offer as an indication that showing gratitude for this was expected of me. In other words, I felt I had to reimburse her for her effort. That's not love, that's a transaction.

Although all of this took place two and a half years before I started my analysis, my relationship with my parents barely changed. My anger about their response to my rape and my realization of how limited they were receded into the background. This was necessary to maintain any relationship with them; I used all my defenses, especially denial. When they demonstrated how difficult it was for them to show their love towards me, I continued to feel that I was responsible for their behavior. I still felt I had to show gratitude for the crumbs of kindness they did show me. It wasn't until this was explored in my analysis over and over again for several years that I fully understood the difference between my limitations and theirs. In my analysis I came to understand why I wasn't initially surprised that they never showed up. What my analysis did that talk therapy might not have done, was go over this material and see it from all vantage points. This allowed me to hold on to my own point of view, break through the denial, and have confidence in my perception of their limitations. When my experience was challenged, I could stand up for myself. My father often told me I was being brainwashed in my analysis. I told him "No, Dad. I was brainwashed by *you*." (Allowing myself to be brainwashed when I was younger was often how my denial was expressed.) It was so important for me to give up denial as a defense mechanism.

After enough years of analysis, I finally understood that even with such an extraordinary event as their daughter being raped, it did not penetrate their usual way of treating their children and they remained on automatic pilot. They responded as they always had: not returning from their vacation when I was sick, not taking any of us to the doctor when we were injured, and leaving us at the motel after we came back from camp. In my analysis I came to understand that I had internalized their behavior and at times responded as they did. For example, during one session my analyst's chair broke I heard the noise but didn't even turn around to see what had happened, nor did I ask him if he was okay. He pointed out to me how unusual my behavior was and I connected it to how similar it was to my parent's behavior at times. Although I hope I didn't do this very often, I learned I had internalized their indifference in this example. I realized the indifference that I grew up with overtook my natural compassion. This incident of ignoring my therapist's potential injury allowed me to connect to my true nature as a compassionate and empathic person as opposed to the indifference I had learned from my parents. This was a significant turning point and I don't believe I was ever that indifferent again. Without the help of my analyst, I would not have been able to both acknowledge that I had the same tendencies or learn to override them.

Not only did I internalize this phenomenon, my siblings did as well. For example, when my sister's daughter needed surgery for breast cancer, my sister was not going to travel a mere hour by plane to be with her. I know how much my sister loves and adores her daughter. This was surprising to me as well as to my niece, however, my niece said to her mom "Really? I'd really like you to be there for my surgery." This prompted my sister out of her automatic response and my sister was there not only before, after, and during the recovery, she was there in any way she could be. This is similar to how I eventually learned to prompt my mother when she made herself unavailable. Once I told her how I felt about it, she would come through. That is how I learned this had little to do with love, it had to do with being on automatic pilot.

I came to understand my parents behavior and take it less personally, despite it being so difficult. As awful as it was to be raped and to fear for my life, my parents behavior was even more hurtful. When there was a reason to confide in a friend my history of having been raped and my parents reaction to it, their response was usually "How could you have anything to do with them after that?" I would respond that one reason was if I were to cut off my relationship with my parents, it would also alter my relationship with my siblings and put them in a difficult position. Although my attachment to my parents was ambivalent, my attachment to my siblings was not. Although I learned how limited my parents were, I also was well aware of how wonderful it could be to be a member of my family. In addition to their weaknesses my parents also had strengths. My parents were not intentionally abusive and they did not mean to be so hurtful. As I mentioned earlier, they were at times very self centered and limited. However, I have fond memories of them behaving differently and of very satisfying and happy times with my whole family. Although I was reliving my rape and my parents reaction to it, my analysis urged me to look more comprehensively at my parents behavior and reinforced that I should not throw the baby out with the bath water.

The anniversary of when I was raped was very difficult for at least the first ten years. The rape and the way my parents treated me became one thing in my mind. I remember my analyst asking me why I wasn't angrier at the rapists. I told him, "I was just an opportunity and there was nothing personal about it." After all, the rapists were strangers. I just happened to be the unfortunate stranger who got into their car. On the other hand, my parents were supposed to love me and show their love for me. I was not a stranger, I was their daughter, yet they treated me like a stranger. I was never as angry at the rapists as I was at my parents. However, because of my need to understand how my parents could treat me the way they did, I spent several years in analysis trying to understand them and I eventually forgave them. Examining and recognizing the patterns from the past that one repeats in the present is a crucial aspect in psychoanalysis that allows the individual to change. This is in stark contrast to a common misconception that much of what a patient does in analysis is complain about their past. Reviewing the past is such an important feature of analysis to prevent the patient from repeating and reliving the past. This enables the patient to create a new and more gratifying future for themselves.

When I finally forgave my parents for their behavior, the anniversary of my rape was no longer so traumatic. Indeed, having learned the hard way that there was more wrong with them than there was with me, it was a turning point that allowed me to not only recover but to heal. It became clear to me how mistaken I was in thinking I came from a perfect family where the only thing wrong with it was me. No doubt we all had our imperfections, especially my parents. To recognize that their limitations were greater than mine helped me to get closer to the person I was meant to be. In fact, I was suicidal for about ten years after the rape. What stopped me from doing it was recognizing that if I killed myself, my father would say "See, I always told you there was something wrong with her." My mother would have felt so guilty and found this so painful that she would deny and never discuss her feelings. My siblings would've followed their lead and I realized I would have been erased. I was not going to let my father determine who I was; a healthy form of defiance. I was not going to be erased. Once I recognized this, suicide was no longer an option. Through my analysis I was able to understand my parents behavior. They did love me but they did not love me well. I no longer consider my rape the worst day of my life. Each year I make a point of going to a special dinner to celebrate as if it were another birthday.

CHAPTER 11

———

Family Life

As I have written in the previous chapter, my analysis helped me to comprehensively examine what my family was like. The previous chapter delineates many of my parents' limitations and how they affected not only me but my siblings as well. However, I would like the reader to know how wonderful my family could be and why I was unwilling to estrange myself from them as many people suggested I do. I would like the reader to understand why I didn't divorce myself from my family after such a traumatic experience and illustrate what my family life was like most of the time. In contrast to the times when my parents were neglectful and hurtful, this was usually mitigated by the family life they created. First and foremost was the relationship they fostered among me and my siblings. They never played favorites and never pitted one of us against the other. They explicitly made it clear to us that our sibling relationship was among the most important that we would have in our lives.

My parents, especially my mother, created a very inclusive atmosphere. They encouraged and welcomed our having as many friends over as we wanted. My mother also went out of her way for us to spend as much time with our maternal grandmother as possible. She lived only seven blocks away and was at our home at least once a week, if not more. We also were at her home at least once a week. All four of us felt very close to her and very loved by her. In analysis I realized the way my parents loved me and the way my grandmother loved me were different. I often felt I had to perform for my parents to get their love. With my grandmother I felt I would receive her love just because I was breathing. Similarly I don't recall my parents referring to me as "*my* daughter" but I do recall my grandmother calling me "my Penny," I explored this in analysis and learned how important this difference was. With my grandmother there was a very strong sense of belonging and feeling very important to her. I felt that way with my parents occasionally when I was with my siblings but usually felt like I didn't matter to them as an individual. I often felt ignored or forgotten by them, as described in the previous chapter. In my analysis when I wondered where I got the strength and determination to cope with the many challenges in my childhood and my parent's indifference to my needs, I attribute it to the abundance of love I received from my grandmother. She died when I was 12 years old and I thought about her everyday for at least 20 years thereafter. I discussed in my analysis what my life might have been like had she lived longer. It's impossible to know something like that but I speculated that I might have had an easier time receiving love.

To illustrate how much fun it could be to be a part of my family, we frequently played board games such as scrabble and monopoly (which my mother often joined) as well as roller derby around the dining room table and wrestling (out of my mother's sight). My mother was a wonderful scrabble player. To this day I remember when I was a teenager she once used all her tiles to make the word *indians* which was placed on a triple word score! My brothers and I were in awe of and proud of this feat. We aspired to play as well as she did!

Here are some of my favorite stories about my family. Often when we went out to a restaurant, the four of us would tell jokes to my parents and we all laughed so hard that the maitre'd told us to be quieter or they would ask us to leave the restaurant. Our enjoyment of one another never waned and was passed onto the next generation. On my 70th birthday, we celebrated in a private dining room at a steakhouse. To our surprise, despite being in a private dining room, the maitre'd came in and told us we were making too much noise and guests were complaining. We were surprised because after all that is why we were in a private dining room! If you had asked anyone in my immediate family what their favorite memories were, we would all have said "dinners." This is a reflection of how much joy there was in my family. The six of us having dinner was always enjoyable and we all remember it fondly to this day. Not only did we discuss what our day was like, we usually played games or told jokes during dinner. This was a highlight of my childhood and I think it was for all of us. We often came up with our own version of television game shows. For example, there was a television program called *Name That Tune* and we did the Mishkin version at dinner. Part of the fun was that my mother could not carry a tune so it was very hard to guess what tune she was singing. Another aspect that was so enjoyable was that we would play the beginning of a song that my father had never heard of so he couldn't possibly guess it. He in turn would sing the first few notes of a song from his youth that we had never heard of, like *Barney Google*. We all had such a wonderful time because the goal wasn't to win, but to have fun. My brother Joe was also a wonderful joke teller and no matter how risque (which wasn't very much in the '60s) my parents loved them. This really bonded us all. Friends loved to come to our home for dinner as they became included in our camaraderie.

Our bonding did not only occur over the dinner table. An instance of family lore occurred when I was 13. One Friday night my parents were out at a party, my sister was doing her homework, and my older brother had friends over for his bi-monthly poker game. My younger brother was away on a sleepover date. I entertained myself, as many young girls do, by playing with my mother's jewelry. All was fine until I tried on my mother's diamond wedding band and could not remove it. I wasn't sure how my mother would feel about me playing with her jewelry because I did not have specific permission to do so that night so I panicked and kept trying to remove the ring. The ring was not tight around the base of my finger, I just could not get it over my knuckle. The harder I tried the more difficult it became and unbeknownst to me I was making the situation worse. I asked my sister for help, to which she responded in true older sister fashion, "Get out of here and stop bothering me! I'm studying for a test!!" I then turned to my older brother for help. I interrupted his poker game, but they didn't mind. They all were intrigued about the situation and how to resolve it. (The silver lining for me was that I had the attention of four of my brother's good looking friends.) We tried butter, soap, and oil to lubricate my finger so the ring would slide off but that did not work. We then tried putting my finger in a bowl of ice water to reduce the swelling I'd created on the knuckle. Nothing worked. My brother's friends eventually left and my brother stayed with me as we resigned ourselves to getting our parent's help when they came home about an hour later. Although I was afraid of being in trouble, my parents were only concerned that I would lose my finger because the ring was so tightly attached to it. I assured them that the problem was only with getting it over my knuckle but the ring was at the base of my finger so my circulation was fine. My reassurances aside, they called the pediatrician at about 2 o'clock in the morning. He told my parents to take me to the emergency room at a nearby hospital. The pediatrician called ahead to let them know we were coming and what the problem was. My parents took me to the hospital. Because this was an unusual situation, the staff were intrigued and they attended to me immediately. I also remember the nurses being interested in this novel ER situation and admiring the ring. They tried to remove it but ultimately it was decided to cut the ring off my finger. My parents were relieved to have the situation resolved however I was worried about how much trouble I was going to get in. My parents were much more concerned about my finger than the ring and they reassured me of that. I was never punished nor was I scolded for this. Their emphasis when they retold the story was on saving my finger. As it turned out (and boy did I feel lucky) the ring was actually a fake. It was the ring my mother would travel with when she didn't want to risk the real one being lost or stolen. I was so relieved. It became a family story told with amusement. *I am realizing now for the first time the distinction between this incident and when I was raped, two situations in which I needed my parents. In the ring situation they felt they were rescuing me from losing my finger, and responded as most parents would: with help. In the rape situation, they could no longer rescue me. It was a fait accompli, as was the case when I was sick. They felt helpless so no help was forthcoming. They did not recognize that even just their presence would console me and make the situation better.* This is an excellent example of how analysis is helpful and continues to be helpful even once it's ended. I learned in analysis how to think differently. I still have insights into my own and others' behavior. Recognizing the distinction between them helping me when they could actually do something was in stark contrast to them not understanding how comfort and consolation was also something they could do. Further evidence that this insight is correct was when I told my mother, many years later, I was getting a divorce. At this point she could more easily articulate her feelings and she said to me "I wish there was something I could do to help you but I can't think of anything." She was acknowledging how helpless she felt. I told her, "Mom, just the fact that you want to help me is a tremendous source of comfort and help."

One of the most retold stories of our family was called "The Bug as Big as a Razor Blade." One Christmas vacation when I was 17 years old, we stayed at a hotel in Florida. It was New Years Eve and I was in the bathroom getting ready for the hotel party. I first thought I saw a double edged rectangular razor blade on the floor. I went to pick it up and as I got close to it realized it was actually a water bug the size of a razor blade. I screamed and the bug scurried away before I could kill it. I told everybody about this bug so they would be on the lookout for it. In the process of getting ready for the New Year celebration, I forgot about the bug. However, after the celebration was over and we all came back to our rooms, I remembered the huge water bug. I got in my bed and could not fall asleep because I had this creepy feeling that the bug was crawling on me. Ricky ignored all my drama and rapidly fell asleep, however Joe, always my protector, tried to help me to no avail. I went to the living room to sleep on the couch, scrunching up to make my surface area as small as possible. However, that was not sufficient to allay my fear. I still felt the bug crawling on me so I went into my parent's bedroom feeling it would be safe there. I tried to be as quiet as I could but accidentally woke my mother who was a light sleeper. She said "What are you doing here?" I replied, "There's a bug as big as a razor blade in my bed. Can I just curl up and sleep on your chair?" to which she replied matter of factly, "No, go sleep in the living room or your bed." I reluctantly left my parent's room and resumed my position on the couch in the living room. I still could not fall asleep. Finally I was so tired I went back to the room I shared with my brothers to go to bed because I was so exhausted. I laid down on my bed and felt something large there. It was my older brother (supposedly my protector). I was startled and said "What are you doing in my bed!?" He said "I felt the bug in *my* bed!" I unkindly told him "Well at least it's not in mine! Get out of my bed and go to your own!" Exhaustion can be a good thing because Joe and I finally fell asleep. It may be important to know that my brother and I had a traumatic history with insects. When I was three and he was five we stepped on a beehive and were stung by most of the hive which resulted in us needing medical attention. Consequently, we were afraid of bugs. Ricky had slept through the entire thing, perhaps because he never was traumatized by the bees. We all had a sense of humor about this incident with the bug as big as a razor blade. Joe told me that when he went on a first date he would often tell this story to amuse his date and gain her interest. When I told my analyst this story (though I don't remember why), he couldn't help himself and he laughed. It was the first and one of the few times he ever laughed in our analysis.

Another humorous story, at least from mine and Ricky's point of view, goes like this. When my sister was around 17 and Ricky and I were around 12 and 11, one night she was out on a date. We knew from previous experience that she would often end the date by going into our living room, the most private public room in our apartment, to what we presumed was makeout with her date. I had the brilliant idea to hide behind the living room couch with Ricky around the time we expected her to be home. Once my sister came home and the kissing was underway, we popped up and said "Surprise!!!" which let them know that we had been watching. My sister was angrier than I'd ever seen her and shouted at us to get out of there. Within a day I believe we were forgiven because we promised to never do it again, a promise we kept. However, karma has a way of exerting itself. Fast forward to when I was 15 and started dating. When I returned from my date, following in my sister's footsteps I went into the living room with my date. You would've thought I'd search the room, but I did not. Ricky made his presence known and it was now my turn to be furious. I now fully understood my sister's reaction when we did this to her. Although I was as angry at Ricky as my sister had been at the two of us, part of me felt that it was well deserved pay back. I'm not sure if my sister ever found the humor in this but Ricky and I did.

I hope these anecdotes illustrate how no matter what the difficulty was, the siblings were there for one another. Situations like this became humorous family lore rather than rifts between us.

There was never anything malicious in the retelling of these stories; we all found them funny and they bonded us perhaps in a way nothing else could. I hope it is now evident why I was unwilling to give this up after how hurt I was at my parent's response to the rape and why I worked as hard as I did in my analysis to repair my family relationships.

CHAPTER 12

"I don't want to belong to any club that will accept me as a member" – Groucho Marx

My first memory of being alone with my father was going to the eye doctor with him when I was 9. As I mentioned earlier, I was nervous about being alone with him because I was unaccustomed to it. I remember I had an early and strict bedtime when I was young and by the time he came home from work, I was already asleep. When I was older and had a later bedtime, I remember he'd come home from work and enjoy a martini with my mother before dinner. Then all six of us would have dinner together. When he was home I only saw him at dinner with my siblings but rarely alone. Even then his face was usually hidden behind a newspaper.

When I was in my first semester at OT school, I was taught to administer the Hooper Visual Organization Test. This is a test which presents the individual with 30 drawings which have been cut apart and the pieces rearranged. The individual is asked to name the object and so must mentally rotate the parts into a recognizable whole. I didn't find it difficult to administer the test however, when I took the test myself out of curiosity I found it very challenging, as the test progressed and items became more difficult. I told this to my analyst because I was convinced I had a perceptual disorder. Given my vision history it certainly was a possibility. He recommended I have a psychological evaluation to assess my visual perception. We opted for a complete evaluation that included IQ, projective testing, as well as various other tests. It was common practice that I not read the report but that the results be told to me. It was felt to be in the patient's best interest not to read the report so the psychologist could be completely honest. My analyst told me the psychologist felt the most remarkable thing about my evaluation was that there was absolutely no Oedipal material in it. Indeed, he said he had never tested someone with that result. I don't know if this was a surprise to my analyst, but it was no surprise to me as I had spent so little time with my father. His presence in my life was felt mostly by his absence.

However I have some other memories which contradict what I've just written. When I was 9 my mother commissioned an artist to paint a family portrait. Rather than having one portrait of the six of us, there were two portraits: one with my father and his daughters and one with my mother and her sons. The paintings were hung side by side in the living room. I remember that for months we all had to pose for the portrait for several hours every Sunday. I hated this not only because it interfered with my weekend, but more importantly because I had to sit on my fathers lap. I sat on my fathers lap while my sister, who was 15, was positioned to sit on the floor in front of both of us. I found it excruciatingly uncomfortable to sit on my fathers lap. Later in my analysis as we were discussing the absence of any Oedipal material in the evaluation, this memory came to mind. I think it was so uncomfortable to sit on his lap because I had never done it before. Additionally, I didn't consciously recognize any childhood wishes for closeness with my father. Similarly, I denied the affectionate feelings I had for my analyst. Although I had dreams about my analyst, I would deny they had any significant meaning. Whether it was my father or my analyst, I felt the need to maintain my distance. When I was 16 my mother took my two brothers on vacation to a golf resort and since I was not a golfer I chose not to go. Instead I deliberately chose to stay to be alone with my father. I even made him dinner on two nights, which was probably a disaster, however he seemed very pleased with the dinners. In addition, my father regularly did business in Philadelphia and I made plans to visit camp friends who lived there and made sure my travel coincided with his. We traveled together by train and it was very special. My father traveled so frequently for business that he traveled in the equivalent of First Class, which was called the parlor car. This was very special because you had your own stand alone (or sit alone) seat which was upholstered and reclined. In addition, we did not have to go to the dining car for food, we had personalized service and it was brought to us. My father was very attentive and I felt it was like being on a date with a charming man who was very interested in me. We both enjoyed his gallantry and I basked in the connection this created. At the two dinners I made for him as well as the Philadelphia trip I got to know more about him as a person. On our return, when we got to Penn Station it was difficult to get a taxi. My father was able to secure a taxi however there was a woman by herself also seeking a taxi. My father asked her where she was going and since it wasn't very much out of our way, he asked if she would like to share the taxi with us. We dropped her off first and she offered to pay her share of the fare but he refused to take it. She insisted so my father accepted it only under the condition that he give the extra money to the taxi driver. I was surprised by his thoughtfulness in offering to share the taxi and admired his solution regarding payment. There have been several times where I've been in the same position and I emulate him.

Another time that was very special with my father occurred when I was 23 and working as a publicity assistant. One of the authors we were promoting was Ed McMahon who was performing at a nightclub. When I told my father this he suggested we go to this together despite it not being my work assignment. Once again he treated me attentively. Other special times with him were the dinners we had when he was in New York on business. Since the young men I was dating could not afford the top restaurants in New York, he encouraged me to choose one of those. I had the privilege of dining at some of the most expensive and renowned restaurants. Once we were dining at a 5 star restaurant and they seated us at a banquette. I was uncomfortable sitting this close to him because he was my father, not my date. There was so little space between us that it elicited the same uncomfortable feelings I had sitting on his lap for the portrait. When I told my father this was uncomfortable, he asked to change tables but the maitre'd could not accommodate us. I asked my father if we could go to a different restaurant. He was very accommodating and we went to another 5 star restaurant nearby. My mother would have criticized me for being so fussy, but my father was impressed that I was not intimidated by the maitre'd and he would often tell this story proudly. As I write this I am getting so much pleasure from remembering the wonderful times I had with my dad in contrast to the negative ones. There were times I was treated like a princess and there were times I was treated with indifference and neglect. This was confusing and no doubt affected my relationships with men. I recognize now that I *did* have Oedipal feelings for my father, but they were so frightening that I had to deny them. This was manifested by there being no Oedipal material in the psychological evaluation and similarly in my denial of any affectionate feelings for my analyst.

I'm sure the evaluation, as well as the memories I've just recalled, gave my analyst insight into how fearful I was of intimacy and why my relationships with men were so problematic. In the first couple dates I would decide whether I was interested in a man or not. If he showed a lot of interest in me, it made me very anxious. I'd become remote and detached and less interested in him. I referred to this as the "kiss of death." Conversely, if I met a man I was interested in but who didn't express as much interest in me, I was more attracted to him. I was either rejecting someone who wanted to spend time with me or pursuing someone who was elusive. I think it's self-evident the problems this would create. My relationship with my father was so conflicted and he was elusive more than he was attentive, that it made my relationships with men very difficult. I knew how to love someone but I did not know how to receive love. To put it in the simplest terms, I was only interested and attracted to men who I had to pursue. When the roles were reversed and the man pursued me and wanted to spend time with me, I couldn't tolerate it and would withdraw. This pattern repeated itself over and over and over again. I strongly believe this derived from the relationship I had with my father. Although I did have boyfriends, the relationships didn't last more than two years. Although my analyst and I worked tirelessly at resolving this conflict, and though we did make some progress, this is the one area in my analysis that I felt was never completely resolved. Another way of saying it is similar to how I titled this chapter; I didn't want to be with a man who wanted to be with me. Although I felt this was a shortcoming on my part, my analyst told me that women with my history of rape and likely sexual abuse in childhood rarely resolved this issue. He asked me if I understood that I felt safer when I pursued the man than when he pursued me because it did not evoke my anxiety due to my history of sexual abuse.

This may surprise the reader but I did eventually get married when I was 47 years old. I distinctly remember being on my third date with a man to whom I was very attracted and who expressed a great deal of interest in me. I remember being in a restaurant where he was expressing his affection. I started to feel anxious and recall thinking *"Penny, are you gonna do this again? You are 47 years old and you are not going to have that many more opportunities. Are you really going to do the same old, same old..?"* My answer to myself was no. I'm not sure exactly how I managed it, but I returned his affection and was determined not to be scared away. We were married six months later and I had fallen deeply in love with this man who I *thought* was wonderful. It is not surprising that three months after we were married I realized he was a conman. During our "courtship", he knew, as conmen know, exactly what to say and exactly how much affection to show to reel me in without triggering my anxiety. I was deeply in love with him when we married and believed it was mutual. After about three months of marriage, I discovered he was frequently lying to me. My analyst was the first person to question some of his behavior. Mixed in with his affection was his ever growing demands to do things his way. In addition, though I didn't realize it at the time, he sadistically lied to me and frequently put me down in front of his friends and family. He was also an alcoholic. Even my analyst didn't realize this before I married him, as my fiance was so good at hiding it. Some alcoholics become belligerent and abusive when they're drunk, however Joel was actually sweeter and more affectionate. When we went out to dinner we would usually share a bottle of wine. What I did not know is that he had already been drinking before dinner and had had numerous shots of vodka. It wasn't the alcoholism that caused me to seek a divorce. It was his lying to me and that I no longer could trust him. I felt once you don't have trust you don't have a viable relationship. I thought if he stopped drinking our relationship would improve. My analyst pointed out that even if he stopped drinking, he wouldn't stop lying and metaphorically making me blind. To illustrate how good a con man and what a pathological liar he was, he remarried before we were divorced unbeknownst to his new so-called wife.

To my surprise I really enjoyed being married even though I had married the wrong person. I liked the intimacy, everydayness, and reliability of it. Following our legal separation, at the age of 50 I dated many lovely men and then hit the jackpot. If I had written down on paper what I wanted in a man, Jerry was the one who fulfilled it. I was physically attracted to him. He was kind, intelligent, considerate, generous, he liked me, and we had a great sexual relationship. He was even an ophthalmologist who graduated from Harvard medical school and understood my visual pathology and its ramifications as well as anyone could. Guess what!? This was too much for me. I felt smothered and his caring made me feel infantilized. Instead of thinking, *here's a man who not only understands my eye issues, he also thinks I'm wonderful and beautiful,* I could not tolerate this. We went out for about six months and throughout that period I discussed the relationship in my analysis continually. I wanted to be able to accept his love and caring, but no matter how I tried I could not.

Three weeks after we met he was my guest at a wedding, and while we were on the dance floor he said to me "I want to marry you." I didn't take this as a serious proposal, rather I understood it as an expression of the depth of his feelings for me. Nevertheless, it elicited all my fears about being smothered and the feeling of *I didn't want to be a member of the club that wanted me.* This was within six months of my legal separation where I had also been attended to and proposed to very early on in the relationship. So I forgive myself somewhat for withdrawing from this wonderful man.

When I discussed this in my analysis, I explained that I was feeling smothered, it was too soon, I didn't want to do the same thing all over again. Jerry was not a conman, he was very sincere but I had difficulty making the distinction because it was difficult for me to trust my perceptions. I wanted the relationship to slow down and I told him that. He respectfully responded to my request. However, when it slowed down my feelings for him intensified. Which then intensified his passionate feelings towards me and I once again felt smothered. This is analogous to smothering a fire with a blanket, which left on long enough will put out all the flames. However, if you remove the blanket in time the fire will reignite. That was what my experience was like when he passionately expressed his feelings; it would smother my passion. I did not treat him as well as he deserved. For several years after the relationship ended, I regretted my inability to accept his love. Ultimately I concluded that if I couldn't receive and return this man's love, I probably couldn't do it with anyone.

I did continue to date but the same pattern repeated itself. I ultimately felt like I was banging my head against the wall and accepted that I was limited in this area. In addition, I was in my late 50s to early 60s which made it more difficult to meet suitable men. I had accomplished so much, overcome so much, resolved so much, and yet focusing on trying to change this pattern was making me feel diminished. I felt that I was focusing on the one thing I couldn't do rather than all the things I had accomplished. My analyst's comment that women with my histories are rarely able to develop a healthy relationship with a man rang in my ears. It was at that point that I considered ending my analysis.

CHAPTER 13

Typical Samples of my Analytic Sessions

Sessions typically began with our greeting one another and then my bringing up what I wanted to discuss. It would then end with my analyst telling me "Our time is up", unless I was in the middle of an important therapeutic moment. As I mentioned in Chapter 1, the frequency of sessions varied according to my needs. We started at three sessions per week and within the first year my analyst suggested that we increase it to four. I asked him why and he explained that I needed more continuity. At this time I was seeing him on Monday, Tuesday, and Friday. He observed that the work we did on Monday and Tuesday wasn't available to me by Friday. In other words, we could not pick up from where we had left off. It was as though we had to start all over again. So we increased the sessions to four a week to enhance my treatment. A few years later when I was reliving very painful material, he suggested we increase to five sessions a week. I said to him, "You want me to come everyday? Do you really think I'm that crazy?"

He told me, "It's not everyday, you're not coming on weekends."

I said, "Well it's everyday you're available!"

He answered very kindly with, "I see how much pain you are in and know from what you tell me that you are feeling the intense pain of your difficult childhood. I think if you came five days we could get through this phase more quickly." I understood his reasoning and also wanted to resolve the necessary issues as quickly as possible. We did return to our schedule of four days weekly when this difficult period was behind me. Similarly, throughout most of my analysis I did not take any medication. Occasionally, when we were working through very painful material I would be on medication for a few months at most until it was resolved. I was never continually on medication nor was I ever hospitalized. It was only psychoanalysis that allowed me to transform.

In another session in the first year of my analysis, I entered and told my therapist the wonderful news that I had won a ten day trip to Europe in a raffle. (That was the first and last time I ever won a raffle!) I wanted to take the trip with my boyfriend who was an associate at a law firm. The only time he could take the trip was in June or July. I asked my analyst if I would have to pay for the missed sessions while I was in Europe since I was giving him six months notice. He said yes. This surprised me because I couldn't understand his rationale. He explained that this was his policy because he found it worked the best for him. I was very argumentative and said "Well it doesn't work best for me. I'm giving you six months notice so it's not that I'm canceling out of resistance or because I don't want to be here. It's just that I have this opportunity for a wonderful vacation with my boyfriend!" He replied something like "That's my policy, you agreed to it, and I'm not going to change it." I became more argumentative to the extent that he said "I feel like you're going to ask me if you will have to pay for sessions after you're dead!" He further explained that he made this his policy because he didn't want to put himself in the position of judging his patient's reasons for wanting to be absent. This is an excellent example of how important it is for analyst's to maintain their neutrality. His explanation made so much sense to me that I finally backed down and accepted it. Ironically, part of the success of my analysis is that I was now comfortable being argumentative! Imagine my surprise and delight when I watched the movie *Annie Hall* in 1977, two years later. Alvy Singer, played by Woody Allen, says, "I was in analysis. I was suicidal. As a matter of fact, I would have killed myself, but I was in analysis with a strict Freudian and if you kill yourself they make you pay for the sessions you miss."[5] (I spoke to my analyst recently and told him I had included this in my book. He told me analysts don't practice this way anymore because they realized it was unreasonable! If only I could get my money back!!!)

Other typical sessions started with my telling him about a dream I had and trying to understand what it meant through free association. I had very vivid dreams and kept a pad and pen on my

---

5 Allen, Woody *Annie Hall* 1977

night table so I could write them down as soon as I woke up in the morning. I learned that some dreams were meaningless because they reflected residue from the activities of the previous day. However other dreams, particularly anxiety dreams and recurring dreams, were more important to pay attention to. I have several examples of an anxiety dream. One, which I think is a common dream, is that it is time for me to take a final exam and I have done absolutely no work for the course. I panic thinking how could I possibly take a final exam when I haven't even opened a book or attended a single class. Another example of an anxiety dream is one I had recently. *I'm not blind when I dream; I see the way I used to see with my contact lenses.* In the dream I had an appointment at an agency for low vision and blind individuals, which was a mile away from my home and a pleasant walk through Central Park. I know Central Park and its different pathways and routes like the back of my hand, yet I kept finding that my usual path was blocked causing me to get confused and lost. I was walking to the east side and could see the trees across the park but was unable to reach Fifth Ave. This was extremely frustrating and frightening. When I awoke and thought about this dream, it became evident to me that because the dream started at the agency for the blind, this dream was likely to be about my anxiety regarding my loss of vision. The obstacles represented my blindness. From time to time I still have similar dreams of getting lost and not being able to find my way home.

The other recurring dream I had in analysis and occasionally continue to have, I've come to call my "intruder dreams." The dream is not always the same but the theme is. Strangers enter my home without my permission and when I ask them to leave, they refuse. I yell at them and threaten to call the police. It doesn't matter what I do, they ignore what I say and remain. I'm completely powerless in this dream. Throughout the length of the dream this repeats over and over and over again. These dreams are exhausting, frustrating, and infuriating. On the surface, this is reminiscent of my experience of being raped. After being raped, I became much more sensitive to intrusion of any kind. In recalling and examining these dreams, my analyst would ask me if there was anything going on in my life where I felt I was being intruded upon. I would thoughtfully consider this to discern what that might be. Inevitably, there was some experience that felt intrusive which we would then examine. I learned these dreams were an indication that there was something going on subconsciously that I wasn't aware of. Once I identified what was intrusive in my waking life, I realized that the dream had pointed me in the right direction.

In addition, sometimes these dreams were very blurry and I found it difficult to see the images. Other times the dreams were very vivid and I saw everything clearly. When I realized this I tried to figure out what that might mean. I had been in analysis long enough that I wondered why some dreams were blurry and some vivid. What I surmised was that the meaning of the blurry dreams was related to material before age 12 when I got contact lenses and the clear dreams related to material from after that period. As a child my curiosity took me to a place where I wondered what it was like to dream if you were blind. Only recently did I get the answer to that question. In seeking help and advice for my current blindness, I was frequently speaking to people who were blind. I asked their permission to discuss how they dreamed. Individuals who are blind from birth and have never had light perception do not dream with visual images. The senses of sound, touch, and smell replaced the visual images. Others told me they dreamt the way they saw in waking life. This makes sense to me because if you have no light perception, your visual cortex is not receiving any information. However, if you do have light perception, your visual cortex will still be stimulated according to how you see.

One day in the middle years, I started the session by telling my analyst my parents were traveling to Europe on an airplane and I was fantasizing about them being killed in a crash. He asked me "Are you perhaps angry at them about anything?" I could've laughed at his question but I took it seriously, thought about it, and told him: now that I think of it *I am*. I went on to tell him that a week earlier before they went away, my mother out of nowhere told me gratuitously that she wasn't going to come to my 40th birthday celebration that my siblings were throwing for me five months later in New York. (My siblings and I had the tradition of throwing parties for each other and our parents on big birthdays.) I had decided to run the New York City marathon, which was the day after my birthday. I asked my siblings to throw a pasta party for me as my birthday celebration and send off to the marathon. I realized I was furious at my mother because she had flown in from Florida for both my older siblings' 40th birthdays. Why was she treating me differently? He encouraged me to confront her rather than hold on to my anger. When they safely returned from their trip, I called my mother. I told her there was something we needed to discuss. I went on to tell her that I was very hurt that she wasn't coming to my 40th birthday even though she had flown in for my brother and sister's. She replied that it was not as nice a time of year and my father wouldn't want to go. (Actually my birthday is in the first week of November and it is a beautiful time of year in New York.) This is an example of my mother doing what she called my father "dirty laundry." My analyst was the one who gave this behavior a name. He told me that my mother often did what my father wanted, regardless of her own feelings. We discussed this at length so I could differentiate between how they loved me differently.

I asked her why she was treating me differently, as it really hurt my feelings. She then said, "You're ridiculous for having your feelings hurt." I finally stood up to her. I told her "No, I'm not. That's a ridiculous thing to say." I think she felt backed into a corner and then said "Why do you believe I meant it?" I replied "Because you and dad were away on my birthday in Europe at least three times when I was a child." She had no response to that. I believe that was the end of the conversation. Whether my parents had come to my party would not have had an impact on how much I enjoyed it. The negative impact was that they were brushing me off just as they did after I was raped. As a result of standing up for myself to my mother, they did come to my birthday party and enjoyed watching me run the marathon the next day. That night they took me and my siblings out to dinner. The next day my mother bought me a personalized paperweight from Tiffany commemorating the time I finished the marathon. Her thoughtfulness with this gift meant a lot to me. I was happy they were there as they corrected their indifference, which they hadn't done after I was raped.

An earlier example of my mother brushing me off was when I told her I wanted to be bat mitzvah'd. She told me I could have one but that I shouldn't expect to have a party or any presents. I expected to be acknowledged the same way my brother was and her telling me that they would do nothing made me feel like a second class citizen. I was so insulted because I felt my mother had no clue as to who I was or what I was about. I liked Hebrew school which was three times a week. On Saturdays, in addition to class there was a junior service run by different classes. When it was my class's turn to conduct the service, I was honored to be given the Torah service. I did not want to have a bat mitzvah for the party and presents, I wanted it because it is a major milestone in Judaism. For her to think that all a bat mitzvah meant to me was a party and presents was offensive. I dropped the subject and then refused to ever go to Hebrew school again. (I don't remember how I ever got away with that but I think on some level my mother knew how much she had hurt me.) Two years later my mother wanted me to be confirmed. In those days it was typical for girls to be confirmed and boys to be bar mitzvah'd. However, I didn't want to be confirmed because it was now meaningless to me. My mother promised to redecorate my bedroom and bathroom if I agreed. I was 12 years old and knew my mother well enough to know that if she wanted to redecorate my bedroom and bathroom, she was going to do it no matter what. This was true because when I didn't agree she did my bedroom and bathroom anyway. (By the way, she did my brother's bedroom and bathroom at the same time without them having to do anything for it.) When I disclosed this experience to my analyst, once again he was able to explain my mother's behavior. My mother's family was more observant than mine. She went to Yeshiva, read Hebrew perfectly, and was confirmed. When she was growing up girls simply were not bat mitzvah'd. He explained that she was probably taking her own experience of not being bat mitzvah'd because she was a girl and applying it to me. Thank goodness feminism came along. I told my analyst what bothered me the most was that she had no idea what good values I had. I wish I had stood up to her the way I did for my 40th birthday. Instead of carrying resentment with me for too many years, I do believe if I had explained what a bat mitzvah would mean to me and how important it was, she would have come around just as she did for my 40th birthday.

Another typical session began by telling my analyst that my father was driving me crazy. I had just graduated from OT school and every time I spoke to him the first thing he asked was "Did you get a job yet?" I told my father I wanted to take a break before looking because my masters degree program had been so intense. I needed a break before starting a new job. He ignored what I said because every conversation thereafter started with "Did you get a job yet?" It was upsetting because I felt he had no confidence in me and did not know who I was. Did he really think after all my hard work I wasn't going to look for a job? *Really?* It got so bad that I asked my father to attend one of my sessions in the hope that my analyst and I could help him understand how undermining he was and how it made me feel he had no faith in me. We entered my analyst's office, sat down, and my father immediately took charge and questioned my analyst's credentials. (This was so embarrassing but I learned in my next session that my analyst understood my father's need to be top dog.) My father proudly went on to tell him that the first and last time he had ever been in a psychiatrist's office was when he was in the army and it was required. He then continued, "The problem with Penny is that she's not more like her mother and her sister." I found this to be an offensive and hurtful comment. I'm not sure if it was necessary for my analyst to see my father's behavior in action, but he could now see first hand what

I was up against. My father and I went back to my apartment and continued our discussion. I brought up other instances when I felt hurt by his behavior. I may even have brought the rape up again. He told me he had no regrets about his parenting and if there was the opportunity to do it all over again, he wouldn't change a thing. I was stunned and I didn't think his behavior could stun me anymore. After that there was no point in continuing this discussion. We then went out to one of our lovely dinners, having compartmentalized our previous conversation.

Writing this made me realize that what was probably at play was my father's anxiety about my future and whether I would be okay. My having a job would have reassured him that I could take care of myself. This is a common concern many parents have for their children. The difference was how far he took it and the tone of his voice. What I heard was that he had no confidence or faith in me. What's clear to me now is that my father was worried about my future. I too felt uncertainty and anxiety about my future, however, it had nothing to do with work. It was the uncertainty of how much vision I would lose and whether I would go blind. When I was 45 I developed visual symptoms that were diagnosed as dry macular degeneration. I went to a retinal specialist and the first thing he told me after examining my eyes was that I did not have the common form of dry macular degeneration. He told me that it was a result of my pathological myopia. He advised me that my symptoms were different from dry age related macular degeneration and I should ignore information about the more typical kind. I asked him if I would lose all my vision. He told me that there was no way to predict that. It could progress or simply stay the same. Initially, I was anxious about this. As I mentioned previously, I had been worried about losing my vision since early childhood but this new diagnosis intensified my fears about going blind. Initially, it was very hard to keep the anxiety at bay. Naturally, I discussed this with my analyst repeatedly and the discussion broadened to the uncertainty that is a part of everyone's life. This helped me deal with the uncertainty regarding my vision but just as importantly helped me deal with uncertainty in general. Ultimately, I came to the realization that if you are in an uncertain situation, you don't know what the outcome will be, so why decide it will be a negative one? I knew it was equally possible for there to be a positive outcome and ever since when I get anxious about something that is uncertain and need to quell my anxiety by deciding what will happen, I imagine a positive outcome. I know that it is possible that I will lose all my vision. However, I try to strike a balance between being prepared for such an event by not denying that it might happen and that I might be very lucky and my vision will get no worse than it is right now. Rather than quelling the anxiety by deciding the outcome, whether positive or negative, I strike a balance between the two. Since I don't know what is going to happen, there is still a chance that my vision will not decline. This attitude guides me through all the uncertainties that life imposes and helps me manage my anxiety.

For example, the world has just lived through an intense period of anxiety because of the pandemic. I was as anxious as anybody about this but kept my equanimity by following all the recommended precautions as well as becoming fully vaccinated. Unfortunately, some people dealt with their anxiety by using the defense of denial and deciding they simply would not get it or it was a hoax. Their denial of the serious consequences of the virus often led them to think they did not need to follow the recommendations to keep themselves safe; they refused to be vaccinated or wear masks and too often suffered the dire consequences. The anxiety caused by uncertainty can also have a positive impact. For example, I recently gave a commencement address in spite of the fact that I intensely dislike public speaking because it triggers my anxiety. However, I find that a manageable amount of anxiety improves my performance and makes me sharper. Even though uncertainty may be uncomfortable, it is a part of life that can bring out the best in us.

A later example of something we discussed in analysis happened after my father died and my mother was rewriting her will. She asked me who she should leave her jewelry to. I replied that she should leave the jewelry to me and my sister. She then asked "What about your brothers?" I replied that my brothers couldn't wear her jewelry and I wanted it only for sentimental reasons. (To this day, whenever I go out I wear something my mother gave me. It makes me feel like she is with me. My relationship with my mother was so ambivalent, the reader may wonder why this is important to me.

Now that she is gone, I emphasize and remember the best parts of our relationship.) I then suggested that she could include a stipulation in her will that if I were to sell any of the jewelry, any proceeds would be split between the four of us. I told her that it felt like she loved my sisters in law more than me. At that point, she was furious and told me "How could you think that? You're impossible just like your sister." *How could I not think that? Given how I was mothered.* At times she was very loving and caring and at times she was detached and indifferent. They both were true, I could only make the distinction based on how she was speaking to me at the moment. I was very hurt by this as I felt my mother underestimated me. I felt she viewed me as being greedy and that is not who I am. My feeling was that if that was the case then I didn't want any of the jewelry. After this encounter, I spoke with my sister as soon as possible and asked her what her experience was with our mother. She replied that their conversation was almost identical. The next session I had with my analyst, I began by telling him about this experience. As I've said before, he understood her more than anyone else. He said that she must have wanted some of the jewelry to go to her sons, and therefore their wives, because that would in turn strengthen the relationship among all her children. She wanted the four of us and our spouses to have good relationships with each other and not have any conflicts. I understood his insight and it changed how I viewed the whole situation. I realized that family relationships were so important to my mother even though it was often at an arm's length that she didn't want us ever to argue about our inheritance. She felt by including her daughters in law, she was ensuring that we would all get along and our relationships would be everlasting.

When my father was dying, I went to visit him in Florida many times. In a very important conversation, he told me that my older brother Joe said he was a better father to his children than he had been to us. My father asked me if I thought this was true. I felt he had handed me a loaded gun. I knew my father really wanted an honest answer or he would not have asked this question to the child he had the most difficult relationship with. Fortunately, I was able to think quickly and told him that no one ever truly knows what goes on in anyone else's family. Although I thought this would be the end of the discussion, he persisted and asked me to be more specific. I then asked him if he thought my brother's children felt loved by their father. He answered, yes. I told him that I did not feel loved by him, and for that reason and that reason alone I felt Joe was a better father. His response to such an honest answer was, "Well you know that isn't true, don't you?" I replied, "Now I know you love me, Dad, but I didn't know it until I was an adult. Especially because this is the first time you've ever told me you loved me. But I do feel it now." I knew he appreciated my honesty. This was one of the most loving moments I had with him and he with me. In contrast to what he said in our joint therapy session many years earlier, we both gave and received love in a way we had not previously.

My father really changed in the last year of his life. As I've mentioned, until then he had been quite remote but as many people do in evaluating their life at its end, he softened. Had I asked him then if he would do things differently as a parent, I think he would've said yes. Indeed he recognized that I too was remote and told me, "Penny, pay attention to relationships. They are very important." When I told my analyst about this interaction he said, "Your father is right. Please don't wait until the end of your life to recognize this."

CHAPTER 14

Termination/Graduation

The concept of termination or graduation from analysis is controversial. Freud called it termination, which I think is a misleading way to describe the end of analysis. I feel strongly about this because the word termination has a negative connotation. At times an analysis does end for negative reasons. However, I was ending analysis for very positive ones. I had grown so much and my life was so transformed that I think of it as having graduated rather than terminated. The only unresolved issue was my difficulty having a healthy relationship with a man. At this point my sessions were only once a week and I would frequently leave sessions feeling upset because we were working on the sole issue that was not completely resolved. As a result, my sessions focused on what I could not do rather than all the things I had achieved. I went from being inhibited, shy, introverted, and very detached from my feelings to becoming uninhibited, outgoing, extroverted, and very in touch with my feelings. If you recall Chapter 1, I asked my analyst how long my analysis would take. His response was *it will take as long as it takes*. In my mind the analysis would end when I was perfect. I learned what an unreasonable standard that was. I had brought up termination in the past when I was angry or fed up and my analyst and I discussed whether it was a good time to do it. As a result of our discussion, I would realize I wanted to end treatment for the wrong reason. However, this time when I brought it up he agreed with my reasoning. If seeing him was emphasizing limitation rather than success, it was quite a reasonable time to end my analysis and consider it successful. Emphasizing what I was unable to resolve implied that I was not good enough, which is how I felt when I first began analysis. In fact the opposite was true. He agreed with me regarding how much we had resolved and accomplished. He even told me that I was more than good enough and we set a date for my graduation which was probably six weeks later.

In contrast to my saying at the end of my first year, "Who me? Miss you? Your absence is of no consequence", we discussed in detail how much I would miss him and how I would handle that. We also discussed that just because the analysis was ending it didn't mean our relationship was. We agreed that I could call him at any time to make an appointment if I encountered anything I needed help with. For example, we both knew that my vision was deteriorating and at some point I was likely to go blind. We knew how difficult and how frightened I would be if this became my reality. It was reassuring to know I could call him if I needed help as I wasn't sure I could cope with this on my own. I recall we agreed that I wouldn't contact him for the first three months unless there was an emergency. This was so I could experience an ending. For the next six months I basked in my accomplishment. I felt so happy to have graduated and to celebrate my successes. My experience of taking delight in my accomplishments in analysis allowed me to use this in my treatment of the children with whom I worked. For example, many parents felt that as long as their child was seeing me they didn't have to worry about the child's area of weakness. However, when I felt a child was ready to graduate from me I would discuss it with their parents and explain how important it is to send the message that you may have had difficulty with something but you can overcome it and enjoy your achievement.

There are analysts who would think someone who had a 40 year analysis was a "lifer." Neither my analyst nor I viewed it that way. Remember, I asked him how long this would take; I always envisioned an ending. I expected it to be sooner but my analyst really was correct when he said it would take as long as it takes. I was proud of myself and what we had accomplished. I was grateful for how my analyst not only saved my life but helped me become the person I was meant to be. This was 8 years ago and over that period I have contacted him from time to time because *I did go blind* but also because I enjoyed updating him on how well I was doing. I had internalized the lessons I learned and now had a different way of understanding others and my relationships. I often felt he was perched on my shoulder helping me to figure things out because I had learned to think like an analyst. Just because

I wasn't seeing him on a regular basis did not mean my analysis was over. In the three years since I have been blind, I have had one meltdown. I gave an obstreperous two year old a run for his money because I threw such a gigantic tantrum when I had trouble putting in my earrings. I made no attempt to control my frustration and had a tantrum where I screamed at the top of my lungs that I did not want to be blind. Despite this, I maintained my sense of humor. My housekeeper was there to help me but I really didn't want her help. I think I really wanted to give in to how frustrating it was to be blind. For the last three years I had been a really good sport. I finally gave in and let it all out. I was now going to be meeting with my assistant for dinner. I did not want her to see me like that so I told her that I was really upset but did not reveal more than that. Over dinner with my assistant, Clara, I analyzed why I got so upset because it had been the only time since I lost my vision that I had melted down. I asked myself as he would have, *after becoming blind three years ago, why did you have a meltdown today?* I figured out by myself that as I was getting ready to go out, I had been fighting the frustration of how difficult it now was to get dressed due to my blindness. It was such a relief to figure this out because it allowed me to control my feelings from then on. My blindness has caused me to let go of certain things I used to be able to do. Rather than fighting it, I must continue to accept it. That is the most gratifying way I can live my life.

I could now recognize how damaged I had been in the beginning of analysis and out of curiosity asked how he knew he could help me from those initial consultations. He told me he just knew. He saw how much strength I had and though at times I let other people define me, I was also tenacious and would not completely accept their point of view. A young woman who not only had survived rape and helped convict the men who raped her must have great strength determination and tenacity. Once we set a graduation date, I gave a lot of thought to how I could show my gratitude. I considered all the ways he had helped me grow, what I had learned from the process of analysis, and how I had learned to think about problems and relationships in an entirely different way. I realized he was my North Star and the best way to acknowledge this in a parting gift was to give him a beautiful compass that was engraved with my gratitude. I explained in an accompanying card why I chose a compass as a metaphor for our relationship. I think he was very touched and gratified, as when I returned on future visits I saw the compass on his desk.

We had our graduation day and I wasn't sure how to say goodbye. It felt like I should hug him or shake his hand or do something physically affectionate, which we had never done before. I asked him, "How do we do this?" His reply was as wise as it usually was. He said, "Let's just do things as we always have." Anything else might elicit new issues!

I left the session and as soon as I exited his building, I burst into tears and cried all the way the ten blocks to my home. I was not embarrassed but I thought people on the street might have thought I had just learned someone I loved had died. When I got home I called and left a message telling him what had just happened and said I knew I needed one more session. I probably saw him the next day and we discussed this strong reaction to what we thought was my last session. He told me he was relieved that I had expressed such strong feelings because he was a little concerned that I had not fully acknowledged how big of a change this was. In the first six months after my graduation, I enjoyed basking in the success of completing my analysis. However, I did miss him. My relationship with him had been among the most positive in my life. Why would anyone deliberately end a relationship that's so positive and important? We were ending the relationship because we had accomplished our goals. There was nothing negative about it.

Although I had seen him occasionally for the pleasure of being in his company and letting him know how well I was doing, several years later I called him out of need. I reached out for his wise guidance because I was now blind. I was grateful that there was someone in my life who understood me so well that could truly be helpful. Before graduating we had discussed and planned for what problems my deteriorating vision might create. I had already lost a great deal of vision. This saddened and frightened me however, he told me that by my age everyone starts to see their abilities decline and I was not singled out as a victim. He reminded me that if I felt sorry for myself I would be choosing to live in victimhood. This reminder was so helpful that when my vision got much worse, I knew I should contact him to help me stay out of victimhood. As an aside, the first time I came back he asked me if I wanted to resume being on the couch or the chair. I was certain I wanted the chair as it indicated the nature of our relationship was different. To this day, I know I can count on him to help me deal with my vision loss. There are other times I give myself the gift of a session so I can have the pleasure of being with him again.

CHAPTER 15

Becoming the Person I Was Meant To Be

When I began analysis I instinctively knew it was right for me but I did not fully understand what I was getting into. I did not know how long it would take or how difficult it would be. I had no idea how much I would change and could not have imagined the person I would become. Based on my initial experience with "talk" therapy, I thought this would be a relatively easy task and did not recognize how deep and challenging the work would be. Through analysis I learned I had more determination, tenacity, and resilience than I was aware of. These qualities allowed me to investigate my issues and myself at a much deeper level which led to my transformation. Sometimes during my analysis some of those qualities went on hiatus. At times I felt it was too difficult to conquer an issue that was holding me back, but I eventually rediscovered my strength.

Throughout my life I was afraid of going blind. When I ended my analysis, blindness was imminent and now it is my reality. I thought that if I went blind I would be completely miserable and helpless. I even considered that if I went completely dark I would not want to live with such a severe limitation. My feelings today are as far away from that as possible. Although I don't like being blind, it's not as bad as I thought it would be. In fact, to my great surprise I am not only just as happy as I used to be, in many ways I am happier. This could not have happened had I not been in a successful psychoanalysis.

Five years after graduating from analysis I became legally blind and was so impaired that I could not read anything, see anything on even a 65 inch television, or go anywhere by myself. At this time I needed all the perseverance and resilience I had. This was at the height of COVID in New York City and hearing ambulance sirens all day long inadvertently helped me put things into perspective. My situation was not life or death although it was very difficult. Years prior, leading up to my eventual blindness I complained to my analyst about my frustration as I was losing my vision. He would not indulge my feeling sorry for myself. Instead he reminded me of my strength and resilience. He also reminded me that everyone has to cope with losses especially as they age and this was mine. Suffering is universal and I felt lucky that this loss didn't happen until I was 70. I had to accept that I couldn't walk any faster than my eyes could see. I had to accept the limitations my disability imposed and adapt to them accordingly. For example, when my vision deteriorated such that I could no longer see the countdown numerals on the pedestrian traffic light, I had to accept that I could not cross when the light was red because I did not know how much time I had to do it safely. Instead I waited until the light had just turned green because I would know I had plenty of time to safely cross the street whether I saw numbers or not. This is an excellent example of how I accepted, adapted, and accommodated to the limitations my disability imposed.

After I graduated from analysis, my vision continued to decline. I did not need to return to therapy because I had already learned how to compensate and accept what was happening to me. I did call my analyst to update him and revisit his confidence in me that I could handle it. I knew, of all people, he understood how difficult this was for me, and yet more importantly reminded me that I was prepared to accept and deal with it. Several months later I abruptly lost almost all the vision in my left eye. Up until then this was the stronger eye that saw well enough so that I could lead a self sufficient life. That loss made a huge difference in my functioning. I was told I needed eye surgery to prevent losing any more vision in both eyes. I consulted with three ophthalmologists who were very skilled surgeons but who seemed detached and unwilling to spend the time to answer questions that would quell my anxiety. Before analysis that would've been fine with me because I related the same way. However, by then I related in a more personal and open way to everyone and did not want a doctor who was detached and standoffish. The fourth consultation was the charm. I had been very lucky to get a timely appointment with the Chairmen of the Department of Ophthalmology at Columbia University, a surgeon who is an expert in treating glaucoma. In addition to being a very skilled surgeon, he was invested in me as a person and not just as a pair of eyes. His warmth and positive nature diminished my anxiety and put me at ease. He was so genuine that I knew I had finally found a doctor with whom I could connect. He took the time to answer all my questions, and there were many, and he empathized with my anxiety about losing my vision and having eye surgery.

My left eye was operated on first and he was so thrilled with the results when he examined me the next day that he repeated several times "This is fantastic!" His pleasure at how well the surgery went led me to share in his excitement and reassured me of its success. I know he was thrilled with the success of the surgery, but I think even more important to him was that he had preserved the rest of my vision as much as possible. When going in for the pre-op appointment for the second eye, which was the eye with the most vision to preserve, he could not find me on his operating schedule. Internally, I started to panic because I was mentally prepared for a certain date and didn't want it to change. I told him that we shouldn't change the date because I had a prayer group set up that included three Jesuit priests. He laughed and said "Oh my goodness, if you have three Jesuit priests praying for you we have to get the date right!" It broke the tension and everyone in the room laughed. Because of my analysis, I knew how to contain my panic and anxiety and was able to joke about this in order to set things right.

When my right eye was operated on a week later, although I was under anesthesia, mid way through the surgery I felt discomfort in the eye being operated on. As soon as I felt discomfort I knew the anesthesia was not working as it should. If I had waited to say something, I might've moved my head from the painful sensation and compromised the surgery. I said "Can I tell you something?" because I knew I wasn't supposed to speak to keep my head totally still. I said "I am feeling discomfort in my eye. Is that okay?." He said "No, we're going to give you more anesthesia." I would never have spoken up before I had learned to advocate for myself as a result of analysis.

This surgery had optimal results as well. Once again I got to share in his delight at its success. This stands in stark contrast to how I used to view relationships with my doctors. I thought their job was to fix me and my job was to comply with their instructions. Because I am no longer so compliant and reserved, it allows for a deeper connection and more mutually gratifying relationship with my doctors. Additionally, without my analysis I would not have pursued four consultations at the height of COVID, all of which were very draining. My analyst was a role model in the kind of medical care I should seek and deserved.

Advocating for myself allowed me to acknowledge my disability and my needs without shame. This was quite different from how I used to be, being ashamed to ask for help. I still talk to my analyst from time to time, sometimes just to chat and in the beginning to get advice about coping with blindness. When I first started adjusting to my blindness, my sister was wonderful and made herself very available to me as she had when we were younger. However, she came to believe that she wasn't helping me enough and I should have a professional who would help me more than she could. I wasn't sure if she was right but made an appointment with my analyst to discuss this. He agreed with her completely and urged me to find the resources that would help me, which were not difficult to find. I contacted several agencies that provided help for blind individuals. I also contacted people who had gone through the experience of going blind themselves, which was a tremendous help. On my recent birthday I made an appointment with my analyst as a birthday present to myself. It gave me so much pleasure to spend time with him again.

When I started analysis I was standoffish and detached. For the first year I kept my relationship with him very impersonal. Through my analysis I became warmer in my relationships, not only with doctors but with everyone. This is parallel to how my relationship with my analyst changed. One of the principles of analysis is to use the personal relationship between the patient and the analyst to change the way the patient relates to family, friends, and other people in their life. Over the years I gradually let myself out of my prison of indifference and detachment. Living without the constraints I learned in my childhood was very liberating. I became comfortable with who I am and very at ease with other people.

I became warmer, more considerate, and openly appreciative of others. *I have realized that it was wrong to view myself as introverted before I began analysis. Rather, I was anxious, shy, and often withdrawn, which could be mistaken for introversion.* As a result of my analysis, my discomfort and anxiety around people disappeared. My extroversion dominates my personality and my life has become so much more enjoyable. For example, last week I went to the bank and all the employees were so warm, kind, and helpful. I told them they are my favorite branch because of how wonderful they all were and they were very appreciative of the praise. Many people, including my previous self, do not take the time to show their appreciation. This not only made their day, but it made mine as well.

One day at my ophthalmologist's office, I commented to the technician who was measuring what little eyesight I had left, that everyone in the office was always very kind to me. She said, "Did you ever consider that we are so lovely to you because you are so lovely to us?" This comment took me by surprise. I didn't realize my behavior was noteworthy, uncommon, or special and I told her that. She then said "Are you kidding? You should only know how unpleasant some patients are." To this day, she makes a point to come see me whenever I have an appointment. This was additional confirmation of how much I had changed from the quiet, reserved, impersonal patient I used to be. Now I genuinely make an effort to thank people for their help and let them know how much I appreciate them. This change in my personality has made my life more joyful in spite of my blindness.

Another example of how I had become my true self was shown in an incident that occurred about four years ago at a bar while I was waiting for a friend to join me for dinner. If you recall, when I was a child and I bumped into someone I often would get the response "What's the matter with you are you blind or something?" I would feel ashamed and devastated. While I was waiting at the restaurant bar for my friend, to pass the time I asked to look at the menu and turned on the flashlight on my iPhone as well as the magnification feature so that I could more easily read it. A man sitting at the bar commented exactly as people had when I was a child "What's the matter with you, are you blind or something?" This time I responded, "As a matter of fact, I am." Rather than being ashamed and hurt, I had put this man in his place and there was no further conversation. It was incredibly satisfying. I recognized that if anyone should be ashamed it was him and not me. People who can transcend their disability and live a productive and satisfying life are to be admired, not made fun of. Instead of viewing disabled individuals as *less than* because of their disability, they should be viewed as *more than* because they are working harder everyday than the able bodied person.

People often discuss whether nature is more important than nurture. I have always felt that it's not an either/or rather it is a both/and. I think we are all born with certain temperamental qualities and inclinations but I also believe your life experience impacts who you become. I believe my natural temperament was to be more extroverted like my older brother and sister. I don't believe I was born being shy, inhibited, detached, and indifferent. I believe I became that way because of the parenting I had, in concert with the impact of my visual impairment. One of the most important things I learned was how much nurture (or lack of it) determined who I was. When I realized how depressed I was in my 20s, I sought a better life for myself. Given my analytical and introspective nature, I was drawn to psychoanalysis. I profoundly believe I could not have changed as much as I have if I wasn't born with the ability to be compassionate and empathic as well as extroverted, uninhibited, and outgoing. For example, when I was young I rarely initiated contact with other people because I was afraid of being rejected. I waited until others sought me out, which fortunately they did. Now I reach out to people, host brunches, and it is gratifying and fulfilling. It is especially important now that I am blind. If I was still as inhibited as I was when I was younger, it would be very limiting because my blindness is isolating enough. Yet, extroversion has allowed me to minimize the isolation my blindness can impose.

What also emerged was that I changed from being a very serious person who took things quite literally to being someone who finds as much humor as I can in any situation. My first job as an occupational therapist was working at a school for emotionally disturbed children. When the staff was gathered together to plan an end of the year party, someone suggested that we go to the beach. Someone else replied that it would probably be too crowded. I piped up and said "Why don't we go on a rainy day? It won't be crowded then." Everyone in the room burst into laughter. Although I knew my comment was humorous, I didn't realize just how funny it was. From then on I deliberately would turn things on their head to make others laugh. I now deliberately use my sense of humor, especially with my blindness, to help others feel more comfortable and to keep things in perspective for myself. For example, I joked my way through my eye examinations as well as my eye surgery. I am lucky that my doctor has a wonderful sense of humor as well. Although I don't think blindness is funny, I do think the mistakes I make because of it *are*. For example, I was at an eye doctor appointment where there were three receptionist stations and I started talking at the first one. When I didn't get a reply, I turned to my assistant and asked "Is there anyone there?" She said no and I found that hilarious. I frequently talk to empty chairs! It doesn't embarrass me, nor do I feel any shame, as I would have when I was younger.

One day I was ordering a new iPhone over the telephone. The salesman asked me what color I would like my new phone to be. I turned to my assistant to ask her what color my present phone was, but before she could answer I realized that if I couldn't tell what color my present phone was then it really didn't matter what the new one looked like. I told the salesman this and we laughed together. He told me this was the best phone call he had all day.

Another example is when I was ordering groceries over the telephone. After I had placed my order, the agent asked me if there was anything else she could help me with. I replied, "Yes! There are lots of things you could help me with but they have nothing to do with your job!" We both laughed heartily. Another afternoon I was entering my building and said hello to the person at the front desk. Usually I recognize who it is from their voice but on this occasion I could not recognize the voice. I asked who was there and he replied "It's Eddie." I then said, "Oh Eddie, I haven't seen you for a long time!" then I quipped "Oh Eddie, I haven't seen *anyone* for a long time!" We both laughed. My favorite anecdote is when I told my younger brother how I tried to pour myself a glass of a very pale white wine. When I went to drink the wine, I was surprised the glass was empty. I was sure there was still wine left in the bottle, so I shook it which confirmed that there was plenty of wine left. Finally my assistant who was nearby said "Penny, you never took the cork off the bottle." My brother then replied, "Penny, you don't have to be blind to do that one, I've done that myself!" We laughed uproariously. In addition, hearing his comment felt so good because it told me how much he understood and normalized my experience. Even when I'm alone I laugh at the mistakes I make. I think it's pretty funny when I mistake an unlit candle for a glass. Fortunately I realized my mistake before my mouth touched the wick! How wonderful it is to become someone who can laugh at herself in contrast to how ashamed I used to feel when making mistakes.

One of the things I love about analysis is that although I changed so much, I still remember my younger self. I vividly remember the reserved, wooden, guarded, private, and ashamed 24 year old I was when I began. I still remember her pain. I'm so grateful that psychoanalysis is a process that allowed me to change even though it was gradual (even glacial). Today I recognize and own who I used to be, however because of my hard work I've become someone I am happy to be. Although everyday I am losing a little bit more vision and am worried about becoming completely dark, I have learned that the harder it becomes, the stronger I will be. With the help of a brilliant analyst, as well as my own personal strengths, psychoanalysis helped me become someone I admire and am proud of. I was able to use everything I was to become the person I am; the person I was always meant to be.

Epilogue

Originally, I was going to write this book under a pseudonym because I wanted to protect myself from the shame I felt as a young person. As I wrote the book and realized how much I had changed, I also realized I was no longer ashamed. Consequently, I was proud enough of what I had overcome to feel pride instead of humiliation. Shame and humiliation are no longer a part of my life. As a result, I believe so strongly in psychoanalysis. Despite being blind now, something I feared all my life, I do not feel diminished by it. I am proud of how I have overcome the challenges it presents. It never occurred to me that I could be just as happy or even happier than I was being sighted. It never occurred to me that my relationships with friends and family would deepen and broaden and be more gratifying. It never occurred to me that I could laugh at the mistakes I make as a result of my blindness. Although I would love to have my vision restored, I am also very grateful for all that blindness has given me. It never occurred to me that the harder it got, the stronger I would become; and the stronger I became the more pride I would have in myself.

Acknowledgments

My grandmother was my first guardian angel. I have been very lucky to have many more than that. My analyst, Dr. Norman Straker, was my second guardian angel. The third, fourth, and fifth are my siblings Phyl, Joe, and Rick for always having my back even when I was a pain in theirs. Once I became blind, my next guardian angel was Rae Covey, who was so helpful and a rae of sunshine. No matter how I felt before seeing her, I always felt better after. My experience with her enabled me to recognize that I could have a wonderful life in spite of my blindness. Clara Chahine is my next guardian angel. Without her I could not have dictated this book or gotten her suggestions that made it better. She is not only my guardian angel because she helped me dictate this book, perhaps more importantly, she is my guardian angel because she is so thoughtful, so loving, so protective, and so reliable. Next I want to thank my wonderful helper Nicole Joly who anticipates almost all my needs. I'd also like to thank my friend and designer Frederick Mayer who has arranged my apartment to make it safe for me and who regularly prays for my eyesight. Next, Harvey Schwartz, M.D. has been an enormous support to the writing of this book; and I have learned so much from his podcast, *The Mind, Body and Soul in Healing*. Finally, I'd like to acknowledge the friends who provided encouragement and support to enable me to complete this book.

www.ingramcontent.com/pod-product-compliance
Lightning Source LLC
Chambersburg PA
CBHW071402120626
46546CB00002B/777